American Language Hub

STARTER
Student's Book

INGRID WISNIEWSKA
ED PRICE

macmillan education

Contents

Welcome

GREETINGS

0.1 **A** Read and listen to the conversation.

Jack: Hello! I'm Jack.
Alex: Hi. I'm Alex. Nice to meet you.
Jack: Nice to meet you, too.

B SPEAK Work in pairs. Practice the conversation. Say your name.

CLASSROOM INSTRUCTIONS

0.2 **A** Listen to the classroom instructions.

1 
Open your book

2 
Close your book

3 
Read

4 
Listen

5 
Listen and repeat

6 
Speak

7 
Write

8 

Ask a question

0.3 **B** Read and listen to the conversations.

1 Student: What does *book* mean?
Teacher: It means *libro*.
2 Student: I don't understand.
Teacher: That's OK. I'll explain it again.
3 Student: Can you repeat that, please?
Teacher: Yes, of course.

THE ALPHABET

Aa Bb Cc Dd Ee
Ff Gg Hh Ii Jj Kk
Ll Mm Nn Oo Pp
Qq Rr Ss Tt Uu
Vv Ww Xx Yy Zz

***a*, *e*, *i*, *o*, and *u* are vowels.**
The other letters are consonants.

0.4 **A** Listen to the alphabet.

0.4 **B** Listen and repeat the alphabet.

0.5 **C** Listen and write the names.

1 ____________
2 ____________
3 ____________

D SPEAK Work in pairs. Spell your name.

A: Hello. My name's Lizzie. L – i – z – z – i – e.
B: Hi, Lizzie. My name's Florian.
F – l – o – r – i – a – n.

1 NICE TO MEET YOU!

A gondolier in Venice, Italy.

> The language of friendship is not words but meanings.
>
> Henry David Thoreau

OBJECTIVES

- talk about where you're from
- introduce a friend
- greet people
- fill in a form

Work with a partner. Discuss the questions.

1 Look at the picture. Which country is the man in?

2 What language(s) do you think he speaks?

3 What language(s) do you speak?

1.1 Say hello

Talk about where you're from

V countries P syllables and syllable stress V numbers 0–10 G simple present *be*: *I, you*

VOCABULARY
Countries

A SPEAK Work in pairs. Say hello. Say your name.

A: Hi, I'm Victor.
B: Hello, Victor. I'm Anna. Nice to meet you.
A: Hi Anna! Nice to meet you, too!

B Complete the greetings with names of countries.

Argentina Australia Brazil Britain Canada Egypt Italy Japan Mexico Morocco Spain ~~Turkey~~

Let's chat! It's easy! It's fun! Click and say hello!

1 Hi! I'm Emine. I'm from *Turkey*.

2 Hello, everyone! I'm Camilla. I'm from ________.

3 Hello! I'm Alexa. I'm from ________.

4 Hi, everyone! I'm Laura. I'm from ________.

5 Hi! I'm Yasmin. I'm from ________.

6 Hi, everyone! I'm David. I'm from ________.

7 Hi! I'm Matteo. I'm from ________.

8 Hello, I'm Emily. I'm from ________!

9 Hello, everyone. I'm Hiro. I'm from ________.

10 Hi! I'm Charlotte. I'm from ________.

11 Hello! I'm Mark. I'm from ________.

12 Hi, everyone. I'm Hamid. I'm from ________.

C SPEAK Work in pairs. Ask about each picture.

A: Where is it? *B: It's in Egypt.*

A pyramid in Egypt

Mount Fuji

Sydney Opera House

The leaning tower of Pisa

PRONUNCIATION
Syllables and syllable stress

In English, we stress a different part of different words. A stressed syllable is loud and strong.

Ar-gen-**ti**-na

1.1 **A** Listen. Underline the stressed syllable in each word. Which word only has one syllable?

1	Argentina	7	Italy
2	Australia	8	Japan
3	Brazil	9	Mexico
4	Canada	10	Morocco
5	China	11	Spain
6	Egypt	12	Turkey

B SPEAK Work in pairs. Ask your partner about these cities. Then underline the stressed syllable.

1	Berlin, Germany	4	Jakarta, Indonesia
2	Budapest, Hungary	5	Moscow, Russia
3	Bogotá, Colombia	6	Stockholm, Sweden

A: Where's Berlin?
B: It's in Germany.

LISTENING

A PREDICT Look at the photo. Read the information. Where are they?

1.2 **B LISTEN FOR SPECIFIC INFORMATION** Listen to the conversation. Which city is the student from?

1.2 **C LISTEN FOR DETAIL** Listen again. Find and correct three mistakes in the form.

Application for Language School

First name:	*Luisa*
Last name:	*Fuentez*
Country:	*Italy*
Phone number:	*07647 293387*

D SPEAK Work in pairs. Ask and answer.

A: Where are you from?
B: I'm from Turkey.

VOCABULARY

Numbers 0–10

1.3 **A** Listen and repeat each number.

0 1 2 3 4 5
6 7 8 9 10

1.4 **B** Listen to Lisa's phone number. How does she say the numbers in bold?

076**4**7 29**33**87

1.5 **C** Listen and complete the phone numbers.

CONTACTS

1 01501 __77 2__9
2 767__ 022 14__4
3 0231 74__ 852__
4 073__ 630 433__

D SPEAK Work in a group. Ask each person for their phone number. Make a list.

A: What's your phone number?
B: It's 07790 521006.

GRAMMAR

Simple present *be: I, you*

1.6 **A** Listen to the examples. Underline the verbs.

I'm from Spain.
Are you from Madrid?
No, I'm not. I'm from Bilbao.

I am = I'm

B WORK IT OUT Circle the correct verb.

am/are		
I	[1]*'m / 're*	from Spain.
You	[2]*'m / 're*	from Turkey.
I	[3]*'m not / aren't*	from New York.
You	[4]*'m not / aren't*	from Toronto.
[5]*Am / Are* you from Brazil?		No, I [6]*'m not / aren't*.

C Go to the Grammar Hub on page 98.

SPEAKING

A PREPARE Read the conversation. Practice the conversation with a partner.

A: Hi! I'm Thomas. I'm from Argentina.
B: Nice to meet you, Thomas. I'm Anna. I'm from Germany.
A: Are you from Berlin?
B: No, I'm not. I'm from Hamburg.
A: Nice to meet you, too.

B PLAN Change the underlined words so the information is about you and your partner.

C PRACTICE Work in pairs. Practice your conversation.

D REPEAT Find a new partner. Practice the conversation again.

Talk about where you're from

1.2 What's your job?

Introduce a friend

V jobs **S** identifying personal pronouns **G** simple present *be*: *he*, *she*, *it* **P** contractions with *be*

VOCABULARY

Jobs

A SPEAK Work in pairs. Which jobs can you name?

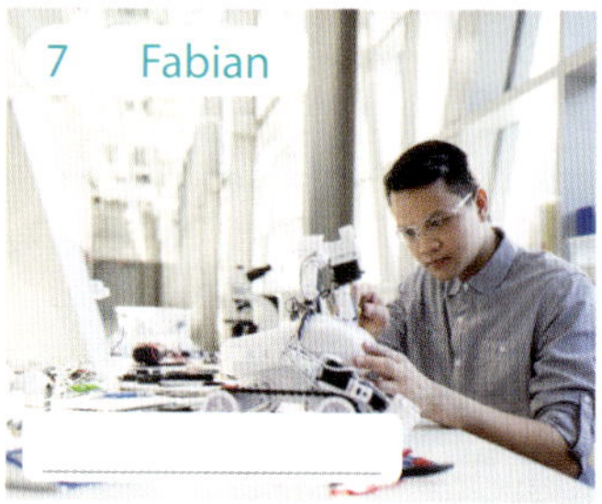

B Match the words in the box with the pictures in Exercise A.

an architect a computer programmer a designer a doctor an engineer a manager a student a teacher

1.7 **C** Listen and check your answers.

D Go to the Vocabulary Hub on page 122.

READING

A READ FOR GIST Read the emails. What is Emma's job?

New job!
To: fashionista@mailhub.com
From: em173@design.nett

Hi Emma,
How's your new job? Is it fun? Is your manager nice? Please tell me all about it!
Keira

RE: New job!
To: em173@design.nett
From: fashionista@mailhub.com

Hi Keira,
Today is my first day in my new job!
I'm on the design team. It's a small team with five people. My manager isn't very friendly, but she's OK. Her name is Amanda and she's from Brazil.
My colleague Anton is nice. He's new today, too. I'm not very busy because it's my first day.
How are you?
Emma
P.S. Here's a photo of me in my new job as a designer.

B READ FOR DETAIL Read the emails again. Circle the correct answer.

1 *Keira* / *Emma* is in a new job.
2 She's on a *small* / *big* team.
3 Her manager *is* / *isn't* very friendly.
4 Her manager is from *Brazil* / *Canada*.
5 Anton *is* / *isn't* new.

Identifying personal pronouns

Pronouns talk about a noun.

My colleague Anton is nice. **He**'s new today too.

C READ FOR DETAILED UNDERSTANDING What do the words in bold refer to? Circle the noun.

1 How's your new job? Is **it** fun?
2 I'm on the design team. **It**'s a small team with five people.
3 My manager isn't very friendly, but **she**'s OK.
4 Her name is Amanda and **she**'s from Brazil.

GRAMMAR

Simple present *be: he, she, it*

A Read the examples from the emails. Underline the verbs.

It's a small team with five people.

My manager isn't very friendly, but she's OK.

My colleague Anton is nice.

How's your new job? Is it fun?

B **WORK IT OUT** Complete the table with *'s*, *is* or *isn't*.

Simple present *be: he, she, it*	
Positive	He/She/It ________ nice.
Negative	He/She/It ________ nice.
Question	________ he/she/it fun?

C Go to the **Grammar Hub** on **page 98**.

D Look at the verbs in the first two sentences in Exercise A. What are the full forms of these verbs?

It's a small team with five people. = It is a small team with five people.

E **SPEAK** Work in pairs. Ask questions about your classmates.

A: Is Anna from Italy?
B: Yes, she is. She's from Milan.
A: Is Raúl a doctor?
B: No, he isn't. He's an architect.

PRONUNCIATION

Contractions with *be*

1.8 **A** Read and listen to the examples. Listen to the pronunciation of *he's*, *she's* and *it's*.

1. He's from Canada.
2. She's from Brazil.
3. He's new today, too.
4. She's really nice.
5. It's my first day.

1.8 **B** Listen and repeat the examples in Exercise A.

1.9 **C** Listen and circle the word you hear.

1. *He's* / *She's* from Vietnam.
2. *It's* / *She's* from Egypt.
3. *He's* / *She's* an engineer.
4. *He's* / *She's* a doctor.
5. *He's* / *It's* OK.

D **SPEAK** Work in pairs. Take turns saying sentences using *he's*, *she's* and *it's*. Listen to your partner. Do they say *he's*, *she's* or *it's*?

SPEAKING HUB

A **PLAN** Student A – Stay on this page. Student B – Go to the **Communication Hub** on **page 128**. Imagine the man in the picture below is your friend. Complete the information about him with your own ideas.

First name ________________

Last name ________________

Country ________________

City ________________

Job ________________

B **PREPARE** Prepare to introduce your friend to your partner. Practice by yourself.

This is a picture of my friend. His name is Ollie. He's from …
He's ________________.

C **PRESENT** Work in pairs. Introduce your friend to your partner.

D **REPEAT** Change roles and listen to your partner's introduction.

Introduce a friend

Café Hub

1.3 How are you?

F– greet people

COMPREHENSION

A Watch the video. Number the pictures (a–d) in the order you see them (1–4).

a ___

Sam's Café

b ___

Gaby's bedroom at night

c ___

The English School

d ___

Gaby's bedroom in the day

B Match the objects (1–8) with the places (a–d) in Exercise A. Then watch the video again and check your answers.

1 ___

books

2 ___

a mobile phone

3 ___

an alarm clock

4 ___

coffee

5 ___

a computer

6 ___

a credit card

7 ___

a calendar

8 ___

a suitcase

C Match the numbers (1–5) with the letters (a–e) to make correct sentences.

1 Gaby is in
2 The café
3 Gaby's coffee is
4 Mark is
5 Gaby's full name is

a Gabriela García Martínez.
b is Sam's Café.
c London.
d a cappuccino.
e Gaby's English teacher.

Glossary

mobile phone **(n) (British)** = cell phone **(n) (American)**

GABY SAM LUCY

D ▶ 01:32–02:28 Watch part of the video and correct the mistakes in the numbers on the form.

ENGLISH, ENGLISH, ENGLISH, AND ENGLISH

Student Registration Form

Name:	Gabriela García Martínez
Phone number:	00707 914865
Classroom number:	6
Teacher:	Mark
Time:	10 am

USEFUL PHRASES

▶ 00:40–01:28 Who says it? Sam (S), Gaby (G) or the receptionist (R)? Watch part of the video and check your answers.

1 Welcome to Sam's Café! ____
2 A cappuccino, please. ____
3 Thanks! ____
4 You're welcome! ____
5 Perfect! ____
6 Can I help you? ____

FUNCTIONAL LANGUAGE
Greeting people

A Complete the phrases in the table with the words in the box.

fine Hello morning See soon

Saying hello	Greeting people	Saying goodbye
1 ________ / Hi.	How are you?	Bye.
Good 2 ________.	I'm 3 ________, thanks. And you?	See you 4 ________.
Good afternoon.		5 ________ you tomorrow.
Good evening.		

B ▶ Watch the video again and check your answers to Exercise A.

PRONUNCIATION

1.10 **A** Listen to the conversation. Notice how the underlined words are stressed.

Anna: Hello!
Stefani: Good morning. How are you?
Anna: Fine, thanks. And you?
Stefani: I'm fine, thanks. See you soon.
Anna: See you tomorrow.
Stefani: Bye!

1.10 **B** Listen again and repeat the conversation. Copy the stress.

SPEAKING

A PREPARE Work in pairs. Practice the conversation in Pronunciation Exercise A again.

B PRACTICE Walk around the class. Greet your classmates.

A: Hi Onur. How are you?
B: I'm fine, thanks. And you?
A: I'm fine, thanks.
B: Great, see you soon.

Greet people

1 Writing

Fill in a form

using capital letters

A Read the form. Where is Alex from? What is his job?

The Global Hub English School

Registration form

First name:	*Alex*
Last name:	*Johansson*
Home (city, country):	*Stockholm, Sweden*
Job:	*computer programmer*
Telephone number:	*451 3398765*
Email:	*ajohannsson@hub.com*

Email addresses

When we say email addresses, @ = *at* and . = *dot* (*ajohansson at hub dot com*).

B Read the form again. Check (✓) the words that need a capital letter.

- ☐ first names
- ☐ last names
- ☐ names of countries
- ☐ names of cities
- ☐ names of jobs
- ☐ email addresses

Using capital letters

We use capital letters for names of people and places.

WRITING

WRITE Complete the form with information about you.

The Global Hub English School

Registration form

First name: ______________________

Last name: ______________________

Home (city, country): ______________________

Job: ______________________

Telephone number: ______________________

Email: ______________________

Fill in a form

Unit 1 Review

GRAMMAR

A Complete the sentences with the positive (+) or negative (-) form of *be*. Use contractions if possible.

1 My name ___*'s*___ Jason. (+)
2 Carmen ___*isn't*___ from Greece. (-)
3 I ______________ an artist. (+)
4 You ______________ in my class. (-)
5 My manager ______________ friendly. (+)
6 I ______________ from Italy. (-)

B Write questions and answers in your notebook using the correct form of *be*.

1 you / from Paris (+)
Are you from Paris?
Yes, I am.

2 Leila / from Mexico (-)
____
____

3 you / a new student (+)
____
____

4 Tony / from Indonesia (-)
____
____

5 Anna / a student (+)
____
____

6 you / Japan (-)
____
____

VOCABULARY

A Reorder the letters to make the names of countries.

1 izrBal ______________
2 yuTrek ______________
3 pytgE ______________
4 adanCa ______________
5 tylaI ______________
6 oMixec ______________
7 nihaC ______________
8 Sinap ______________
9 apJan ______________
10 natrAnige ______________

B Complete the jobs with the missing letters.

1 d __ c __ or
2 computer p __ og __ __ m __ __ r
3 ar __ h __ __ e __ t
4 e __ __ i __ e __ r
5 fashion d __ __ i __ n e __
6 t __ __ c __ __ r

2 OUR MUSIC, OUR WORLD

> Music is the universal language of mankind.
>
> Henry Wadsworth Longfellow

Musicians playing in a mariachi band, Guanajuato, Mexico.

OBJECTIVES

- talk about nationalities
- ask for and give personal information
- ask for clarification
- write an online introduction

Work with a partner. Discuss the questions.

1 Look at the picture. What type of music is it?

2 Choose two words to describe the picture.

boring happy interesting
modern sad traditional

3 What do you think the quote means?

2.1 Where are they from?

Talk about nationalities

V languages and nationalities **P** syllable stress **G** simple present *be*: *we*, *you*, *they*; possessive adjectives

READING

A SCAN FOR INFORMATION Look at the pictures. Read the playlist. Where are the people from?

World Music fans!
Are you ready for some great new music?
On our playlist this week ...

Esperanza Spalding is a musician from Portland in the US. She's 33 years old and she's a jazz musician. Her songs are in English, **Spanish** and **Portuguese**. We're big fans of her new album!

Fatoumata Diawara is a singer and musician from **Mali**. She's 36 years old and a big star in Africa. Her album *Fatou* is one of our favorites, and our new favorite song is *Fenfo* from the new album *Fenfo* (*Something to Say*)!

Of Monsters and Men is a band of five people. They're from Reykjavík in Iceland. Their songs are really fun but they aren't in **Icelandic** – they're in English.

Monoswezi is an international band. Two of the band members are **Swedish**, one is **Norwegian**, one is from Mozambique and one is from Zimbabwe. Their music is a mix of African and European music. These musicians are super cool!

B READ FOR DETAIL Read the playlist and check (✓) the correct name.

	Esperanza Spalding	Fatoumata Diawara	Of Monsters and Men	Monoswezi
1 The people in this band are from one country.	☐	☐	☐	☐
2 Her songs are in three languages.	☐	☐	☐	☐
3 The people in this band are from different countries.	☐	☐	☐	☐
4 Their music is a mix of music from different countries.	☐	☐	☐	☐
5 This singer is from the US.	☐	☐	☐	☐
6 She's a big star in Africa.	☐	☐	☐	☐

C SPEAK Work in pairs. Which musicians in the playlist do you want to listen to?

VOCABULARY

Languages and nationalities

A Read the playlist again. Complete the languages and nationalities.

	Country	Language/Nationality
1	Spain	Spanish
2	Portugal	________
3	Iceland	________
4	Sweden	________
5	Norway	________

B Work in pairs. Write the nationalities of these musicians. Choose an ending from the box.

~~-ese~~ -ian -ish

1 Midori is from Japan. She's Japan*ese*.
2 Marisa Monte is from Brazil. She's Brazil________.
3 Bono is from Ireland. He's Ir________.

C Go to the Vocabulary Hub on page 122.

1

2

PRONUNCIATION
Syllable stress

.1 **A** Listen to the countries and nationalities. Underline the stressed syllables in the nationalities. Do the countries and nationalities have the same or different stress?

1 Sweden Swedish *same / different*
2 Egypt Egyptian *same / different*
3 Iceland Icelandic *same / different*

.1 **B** Listen again and repeat.

.2 **C** Listen and underline the stressed syllable in each country and nationality. Is the stress the same or different?

1 China – Chinese *same / different*
2 Turkey – Turkish *same / different*
3 Canada – Canadian *same / different*
4 Poland – Polish *same / different*
5 Italy – Italian *same / different*

.2 **D** Listen and repeat.

E SPEAK Work in pairs. Add another country and nationality for each ending.

Country	Nationality
1 ______	______ese
2 ______	______ish
3 ______	______(i)an

GRAMMAR
Simple present *be: we, you, they*

A Read the examples from the playlist. Underline the verbs.

Are you ready for some great new music?
They're from Reykjavík in Iceland.
… but they aren't in Icelandic – they're in English.
We're big fans of her new album.

B WORK IT OUT Complete the table with the positive and negative forms of the verb *be*.

Subject	Positive	Negative
I	'm / am	'm not
you	're / are	aren't
he/she/it	's / is	isn't
we	______	______
you	______	______
they	______	______

C Go to the Grammar Hub on page 100.

D SPEAK Complete the questions. Then ask and answer them with your partner.

1 *Are / Is* you a fan of world music?
2 *Are / Is* your favorite musicians from America?

Possessive adjectives

A Read the examples. Underline the possessive adjectives.

On our playlist this week …
Their songs are really fun.
We're big fans of her new album!

B WORK IT OUT Complete the table with possessive adjectives from the box.

Her His Its ~~My~~ Our Their Your

Subject pronoun	Possessive adjective
I am a world music fan.	1 ___My___ name is Luciana.
You are from Brazil.	2 ______ songs are in Portuguese.
She is a singer from Mali.	3 ______ songs are sad.
He is from Sweden.	4 ______ songs are in Swedish.
This is the new album.	5 ______ name is *Fenfo*.
We are world music fans.	6 ______ playlist is cool.
They are from Iceland.	7 ______ music is full of energy.

C PRACTICE Circle the correct possessive adjective.

1 They're in a band. *Her / Their* new album is great.
2 We're fans of great music. *Our / Their* favorite music is from Brazil.
3 She's a musician. *His / Her* name is Ariane.
4 He's a singer. *Her / His* name is Michael.

D Go to the Grammar Hub on page 100.

SPEAKING

A PREPARE Write information about your favorite musician or band.

Name: ______
Country: ______
Age: ______
Name of album or song: ______
______

B DISCUSS Work in pairs. Tell your partner about your favorite musician or band.

C REPORT Tell the class about your partner's favorite musician or band.

Talk about nationalities

2.2 When are you free?

Ask for and give personal information

V – days of the week; numbers 11–100 S – identifying context G – *wh-* questions with *be* P – contractions in questions

VOCABULARY

Days of the week

A Read the flyer. Which class looks fun?

INTERNATIONAL CENTER

ADULT EVENING CLASSES

Learn something new!
Learn about other cultures and meet people!

All classes start at 7 pm

MONDAY
Spanish guitar classes
60 mins Room 8

TUESDAY
African drums workshop
75 mins Room 24

WEDNESDAY
Arabic language class
90 mins Room 12

THURSDAY no classes

FRIDAY
Yoga for everyone
45 mins Room 18

SATURDAY AND SUNDAY no classes

2.3 **B** Listen and repeat the days of the week.

C SPEAK Work in pairs. Ask your partner questions about the classes.

A: What day is yoga?
B: Friday!

Numbers 11–100

2.4 **A** Listen and repeat the numbers. Notice the stressed syllable.

11 eleven	20 twenty
12 twelve	30 thirty
13 thirteen	40 forty
14 fourteen	50 fifty
15 fifteen	60 sixty
16 sixteen	70 seventy
17 seventeen	80 eighty
18 eighteen	90 ninety
19 nineteen	100 one hundred

B Go to the Vocabulary Hub on page 122.

2.5 **C** SPEAK Work in pairs. Circle all the numbers in the flyer and say them with your partner. Then listen and check.

LISTENING

2.6 **A** LISTEN FOR GIST Listen to three conversations. Write the number of the conversation.

Who are they?

a teachers ______
b students ______
c friends *Conversation 1*

1

2

3

Identifying context

Greetings such as *Good morning* or *Good afternoon* are more formal.

Hi! and *Hello!* are less formal.

2.6 **B** LISTEN FOR DETAIL Match the greetings in the box with the conversations (1–3).

Good afternoon! Hello! Hi!
Nice to meet you! (x2)

2.6 **C** LISTEN FOR DETAIL Listen again. Choose the correct answers to complete the sentences.

1 Kara's teacher is …
  a Spanish. **b** Argentinian.
2 Maria and Angelo are in classroom …
  a 12B. **b** 12C.
3 Maria and Angelo are in …
  a a Spanish class. **b** an Arabic class.
4 Leila is …
  a the Arabic teacher. **b** the yoga teacher.

GRAMMAR

Wh- questions with *be*

A Read the examples. Underline the question words.

What's your name?
Who's your teacher?
Where's she from?
When are you free?
How old are you?

B **WORK IT OUT** Choose the correct word to complete the questions.

1 **What / Who** are their jobs?
2 **When / How** old are Kara and Pete?
3 **What / Where** are they from?
4 **What / Who** is your teacher?
5 **When / What** is your Spanish class?

C **WORK IT OUT** Choose the correct options to complete the rules.

wh-* questions with *be

1 In *wh-* questions, the ***verb* / *question word*** is first.
2 In *wh-* questions, the ***verb* / *question word*** is second.

D Go to the **Grammar Hub** on **page 100**.

E **PRACTICE** Complete the questions with the correct form of the verb *be*. Then match the questions (1–5) with the answers (a–e).

1 What ________ their names?
2 Where ________ she from?
3 When ________ your yoga classes?
4 How old ________ your children?
5 Who ________ your favorite musicians?

a 5 and 8
b Lucia and Stefan
c On Fridays
d Of Monsters and Men and Coldplay
e Australia

F **SPEAK** Work in pairs. Use the prompts to ask and answer the questions.

1 When / your (English) classes?
2 Who / your teacher?
3 Where / your teacher from?

PRONUNCIATION

Contractions in questions

2.7 **A** Read and listen to these questions. Notice how *who* and *how* are pronounced.

1 Who's your teacher?
2 How's your teacher?
3 Who are you?
4 How are you?

2.7 **B** Listen and repeat the examples in Exercise A.

2.8 **C** Listen and choose the correct answer to the questions you hear.

1 **a** He's Mr. Parker. **b** He's really nice.
2 **a** I'm a new student. **b** I'm fine, thank you.
3 **a** She's OK, thank you. **b** Her name's Anna.
4 **a** This is Pedro and this is Yuki. **b** They're great!

D **SPEAK** Work in pairs. Write four questions using *Who's*, *How's*, *Who are* and *How are*. Then ask your partner.

SPEAKING HUB

A **PREPARE** Work in pairs. Student A – Stay on this page. Student B – Go to the **Communication Hub** on **page 132**.

Read the information. What questions can you ask to find the missing information?

1 *What's his name?*
2 ________?
3 ________?
4 ________?
5 ________?
6 ________?
7 ________?
8 ________?

B **PRACTICE** Ask your partner your questions from Exercise A to complete the information about each person.

a

Name	1 ________
Country	Argentina
Age	2 ________
Job	Designer

b

Name	Tomoko Kogawa
Country	3 ________
Age	35
Job	4 ________

c

Name	5 ________
Country	India
Age	6 ________
Job	Engineer

d

Name	7 ________
Country	Turkey
Age	25
Job	8 ________

Ask for and give personal information

Café Hub

2.3 I'm late

F– ask for clarification

COMPREHENSION

A Watch the video. Number the pictures (a–h) in the order you see them (1–8).

a ____

b ____

c ____

d ____

e ____

f ____

g ____

h ____

B Complete the information in the table. Watch the video again and check your answers.

Name	Gaby	3 ______	4 ______	Onur	7 ______
Nationality	1 ______	English	5 ______	6 ______	Italian
Job	2 ______	English teacher	primary school teacher	student	8 ______

USEFUL PHRASES

A Who says it? Gaby (G), Mark (M) or Carolina (C)? Watch the video again and check your answers.

1 Please sit down. ______

2 Yes, that's it. ______

3 Nice to meet you. ______

4 Hi, guys. ______

5 Now it's your turn. ______

6 I'm late! ______

B Student A – Mime a phrase in Exercise A. Student B – Say the phrase. Then change roles.

GABY

SAM

LUCY

FUNCTIONAL LANGUAGE

Asking for clarification

A Complete the phrases with the verbs in the box.

mean say understand

1 Carolina: How do you [1] ________ *primário* in English?
Mark: 'Primary', I think.

2 Marta: I'm a nurse.
Carolina: I'm sorry, I don't [2] ________.

3 Onur: What does 'nurse' [3] ________?
Mark: *Enfermeira*

B 02:01–02:50 Watch part of the video and check your answers to Exercise A.

C Reorder the words to make the phrases.

1 mean? / What / 'student' / does

____

2 you / say / in English? / How / do / *obrigado*

____

3 understand. / I'm sorry, / I / don't

____

PRONUNCIATION

A 2.9 Listen to the conversation. Notice how the underlined words are stressed.

Angela: Good morning, everyone. My name's Angela. I'm your English teacher.

Roberto: I'm Roberto. I'm from Italy. How do you say *medico* in English?

Angela: 'Doctor'.

Roberto: Oh yes, that's it. I'm a doctor.

Monika: Hi. My name's Monika. I'm Polish and I'm an architect.

Roberto: I'm sorry, I don't understand. What does 'architect' mean?

B 2.9 Listen again and repeat the conversation. Copy the stress.

SPEAKING

A PREPARE You are going to introduce yourself to a group. Think about what you want to say.

- name
- nationality
- job

B PRACTICE Work in groups. Imagine you are in a new class. Practice your conversation.

C PRESENT Perform your conversation for the rest of the class.

Glossary

primary school teacher (n) (British) = elementary school teacher (n) (American)

Ask for clarification

2 Writing — Write an online introduction

W — using *and* to join sentences

A Read the title and introduction of the blog post. What do you think Tina writes about?

address age birthday country job name nationality phone number teacher's name

GLOBAL HUB LANGUAGE SCHOOL

Home Forum About Login Sign up

Say hello to your classmates.
Post your introductions on this page.

Posted by: Tina Gonzalez

Hi, everyone! My name's Tina and I'm from Mexico. I'm 28 years old and I'm a photographer. My English classes are on Tuesdays and Thursdays. My teacher is Mr. Sampson. He's from Ottawa in Canada. I'm a big fan of British music. My favorite bands are Coldplay and Arctic Monkeys. Their music is really cool!

Using *and* to join sentences

We use *and* to link ideas. *And* gives extra information.

I'm 28 years old *and* I'm a new student.

B Read Tina's self-introduction again. Answer the questions.

1 Where's Tina from? ____________
2 How old is she? ____________
3 What's her job? ____________
4 Who's Mr. Sampson? ____________
5 Who are her favorite bands? ____________

WRITING

A PLAN Imagine you are at a new school. Complete the information.

What's your name?	
Where are you from?	
What's your job?	
When are your English classes?	
Who's your teacher?	
Who are your favorite musicians?	

B WRITE Write an introduction for your school web forum. Use Tina's introduction to help you. Use *and* to join sentences.

○ Write an online introduction

Unit 2 Review

GRAMMAR

A Choose the correct verb to complete the sentences.

1 We *am* / *is* / *are* from Morocco.
2 My friend *am* / *is* / *are* Portuguese.
3 *Am* / *Is* / *Are* you a fan of world music?
4 Their names *am* / *is* / *are* Paolo and Pawel.

B Write the questions for these answers.

1 He's a teacher. *What's his job?*
2 They're from Brazil. ____________
3 Her name is Elise. ____________
4 My class is on Thursday. ____________
5 I'm 34 years old. ____________
6 My teacher is Mr. Stevens. ____________

C Circle the correct possessive adjectives.

1 She's from Brazil and *his* / *her* songs are in Portuguese.
2 We're from Iceland, but *our* / *their* songs are in English.
3 They're from Senegal and *our* / *their* music is traditional.
4 You're from Mexico, but *my* / *your* name is German.

VOCABULARY

A Write the nationalities for these countries.

1 Brazil *Brazilian*
2 Canada ____________
3 Iceland ____________
4 Turkey ____________
5 Egypt ____________
6 Poland ____________
7 Japan ____________
8 Argentina ____________

B Complete the days of the week.

1 M _ _ d a y
2 T _ _ s d a y
3 W _ d _ _ _ d a y
4 T _ u _ _ d a y
5 F _ _ d a y
6 S _ t _ _ d a y
7 S _ _ d a y

3 MY LIFE

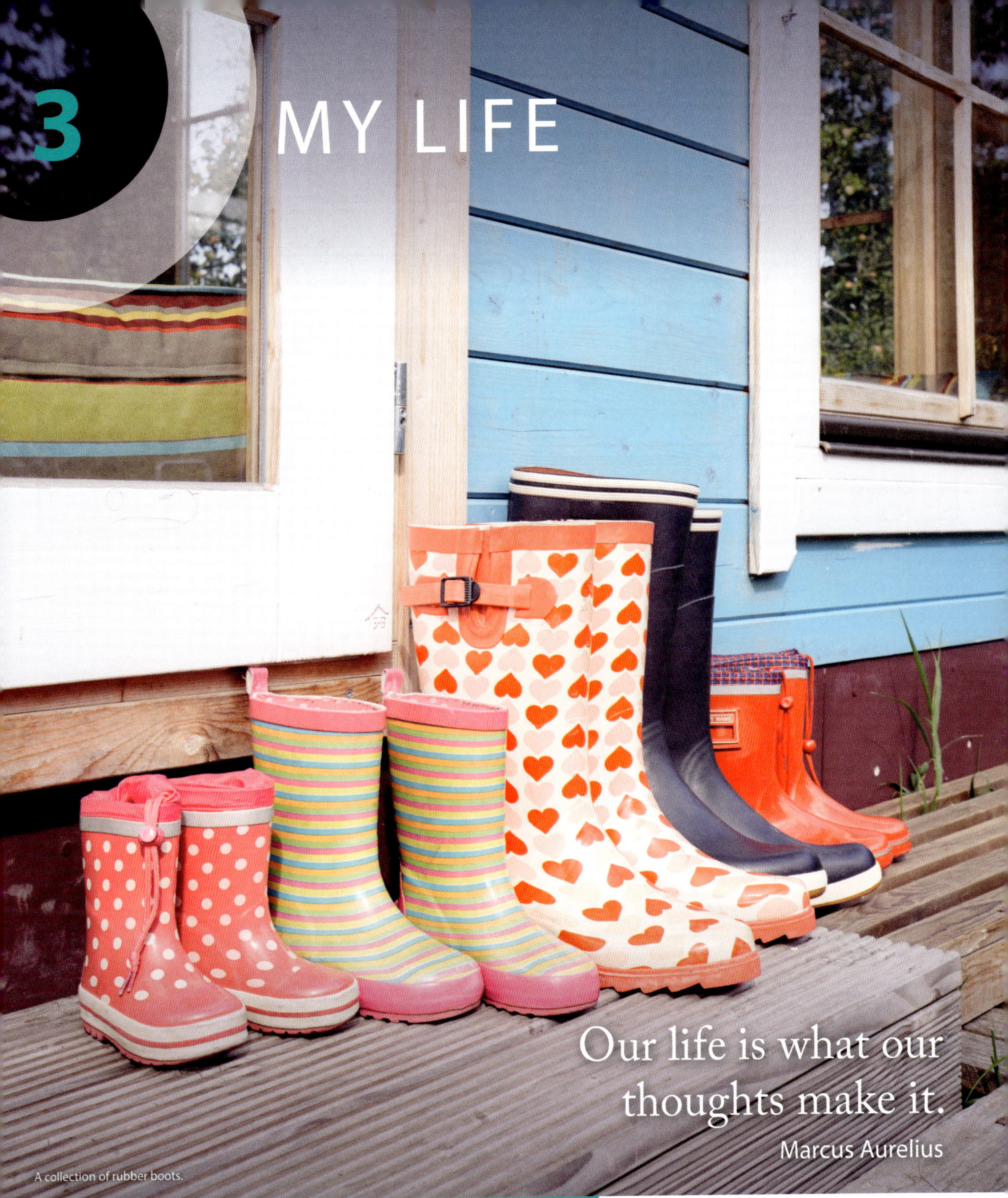

Our life is what our thoughts make it.

Marcus Aurelius

A collection of rubber boots.

OBJECTIVES

- describe everyday objects
- talk about your family
- describe people
- write a social media post

Work with a partner. Discuss the questions.

1 Choose words that match the picture.

family home job nationality school

2 Who do you think lives in the house?

3 Who is important in your life?

3.1 That's my coat

Describe everyday objects

V objects and colors G *a/an* and plural nouns; *this, that, these, those* P /s/, /z/ and /ɪz/

VOCABULARY
Objects and colors

A Look at the picture. Write the letter (or letters) for these words.

a hat ___
a phone ___
a sweatshirt ___
an umbrella ___
a bag *a*, ___, ___, ___
a coat ___, ___, ___, ___
glasses ___
headphones ___

B Look at the picture again. Write the correct letter.

Which coat is …

1 blue? ___
2 red? ___
3 green? ___
4 black? ___

C Go to the **Vocabulary Hub** on **page 123**.

C SPEAK Work in pairs. Say the color and name of an object in the picture. Your partner says the correct letter.

A: A blue bag
B: Letter c!
A: Correct. White glasses …

GRAMMAR
a/an and plural nouns

A WORK IT OUT Read the examples. Choose the correct options for the sentences in the box.

In the picture, …
letter j is a sweatshirt.
letter i is an umbrella.
letters k, l, m, and n are coats.

***a/an* and plural nouns**

1 We use *a/an* when there is *one / more than one* object.
2 We add *s* when there is *one / more than one* object.

B Go to the **Grammar Hub** on **page 102**.

PRONUNCIATION
/s/, /z/ and /ɪz/

3.1 **A** Listen and repeat the sounds and the words.

/s/ coats   /z/ headphones   /ɪz/ glasses

3.2 **B** Listen to the words. Choose the correct sound for the underlined letters.

1 umbrellas /s/ /z/ /ɪz/
2 hats /s/ /z/ /ɪz/
3 bags /s/ /z/ /ɪz/
4 classes /s/ /z/ /ɪz/

C SPEAK Work in pairs. Make a list of the objects from Vocabulary Exercise A that are in your classroom. Say how many.

A: an umbrella
B: sixteen black bags

LISTENING

3.3 **A LISTEN FOR GIST** Listen to the conversation. What is the problem?

3.3 **B LISTEN FOR KEY WORDS** Listen again. Look at the picture above and circle all the objects that you hear.

3.3 **C LISTEN FOR DETAIL** Listen again and answer the questions.

1 What's the woman's ticket number? ___
2 What color is the woman's coat? ___
3 What color are the woman's bags? ___ / ___

GRAMMAR

this, that, these, those

3.4

A Look at the pictures. Listen and complete the sentences from the conversation with *this, that, these* or *those*.

a

Coatroom attendant:	Is [1] ________ your coat?
Customer:	No! My coat is blue. [2] ________ coat is green.

b

Coatroom attendant:	Are [3] ________ your bags?
Customer:	No! [4] ________ bags are red and blue.

B WORK IT OUT Look at the pictures and sentences in Exercise A again. Match the numbers (1–4) with the letters (a–d) to complete the rules.

this, that, these, those

1 We use *this* and *that* to talk about …
2 We use *these* and *those* to talk about …
3 We use *this* and *these* to talk about …
4 We use *that* and *those* to talk about …

a more than one object.
b things that are not near.
c one object.
d things that are near.

C Go the Grammar Hub on page 102.

D PRACTICE Write *this, that, these* or *those* and the name of the object for each picture.

1 ________________

2 ________________

3 ________________

4 ________________

SPEAKING

A PRACTICE Work in pairs. Practice the conversation.

Customer:	Can I have my hat, please?
Coatroom attendant:	Is this your hat?
Customer:	No. That hat is blue. My hat is green.
Coatroom attendant:	Is this your hat?
Customer:	Yes, that's my hat.

B PREPARE Work in groups. You are going to ask for your own objects at a coatroom.

One person is the coatroom attendant. Go to the Communication Hub on page 129.

The rest of the group are customers.

- Put some objects on the table. Try and put out more than one of the same type of object.
- Think about the names of the objects (hat, bag, headphones, etc).
- Think about the colors (red, blue, black, white, gray, brown, etc).
- Don't tell the attendant which object is yours.

Remember: *that/those.*

C DISCUSS Ask for your things at the coatroom. Use the conversation in Exercise A to help you.

D REPEAT Change roles and repeat.

A: Can I have my glasses, please?
B: Are these your glasses?
A: No, they aren't. Those glasses are brown. My glasses are black.

Describe everyday objects

3.2 I have two sisters

Talk about your family

S finding key information V family P schwa /ə/ G *have/has*

READING

A PREPARE TO READ Look at the picture. Choose three words from the box to describe it.

cake family job party restaurant

100 YEARS YOUNG!

Local woman celebrates her 100th <u>birthday</u> with her family.

Lilly Wenders is 100 years old this week, and there's a family party to celebrate. 'A lot of my family lives in the same <u>town</u> as me,' says Lilly. 'I'm very lucky.'

Lilly is not the oldest person in her family. She has two **sisters**. Agatha is 103 and Hattie is 106.

Lilly has two **children**, Sally and Emily, and three **grandchildren**: Katrina, Olivia and Clara. 'I don't have a **son** or a **grandson**,' says Lilly. 'My children and my grandchildren are all <u>women</u>.'

'Do you have any men in your family?' I ask Lilly.

'Yes, I do,' says Lilly. 'I have a **husband**, Arthur. It's his birthday this week, too, but he's only 84!'

Finding key information

Finding the important information first can help you to understand a text.

Examples of important information are:

- names (people, places)
- numbers (age, time, date)

B SCAN FOR INFORMATION Read the article quickly. Match the people (1–4) with their ages (a–d).

1 Lilly	a 84
2 Agatha	b 100
3 Hattie	c 103
4 Arthur	d 106

C READ FOR DETAIL Read the article again. Complete the statements with the <u>underlined</u> words in the article.

1 The party is for Lilly's ______________.

2 Lilly lives in the same ______________ as a lot of people in her family.

3 Lilly has a lot of ______________ in her family.

D SPEAK Work in pairs. Answer the questions.

1 Do you know anyone who is 100 years old?

2 Do you live in the same town/city as your family?

VOCABULARY

Family

A Find the words in bold in the article. Put them in the correct place in the table.

Female	Male
mother	father
1 ______________	brother
daughter	2 ______________
grandmother	grandfather
granddaughter	3 ______________
wife	4 ______________
Female and/or male	
parents	
5 ______________	6 ______________

B Complete the family tree with names from the article.

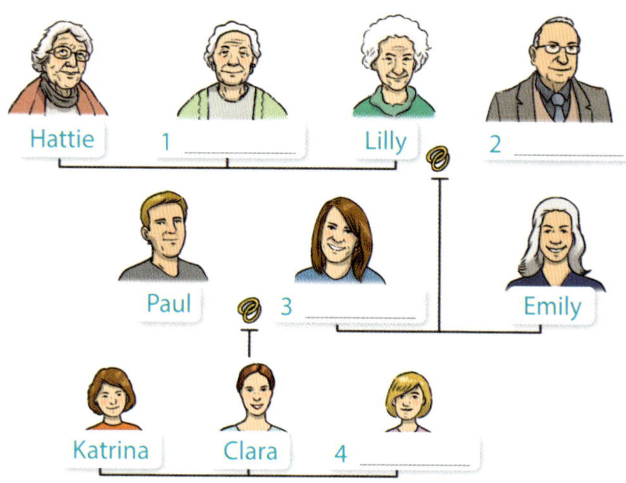

C Complete the sentences with words from Exercise A.

1 Arthur: 'Lilly is my ______________.'

2 Hattie: 'Lilly is my ______________.'

3 Emily: 'Lilly is my ______________.'

4 Clara: 'Lilly is my ______________.'

PRONUNCIATION
schwa /ə/

3.5 **A** Listen to the sentences. Notice how the underlined letters sound.

1 Lilly is my mother. 3 Paul is my husband.
2 Arthur is my father. 4 I have three children.

3.5 **B** Listen again and repeat.

3.6 **C** Underline the letters with the schwa sound. Listen and check.

1 daughter 2 parents 3 grandfather 4 brother

D Connect the words with the schwa sound to get out of the maze.

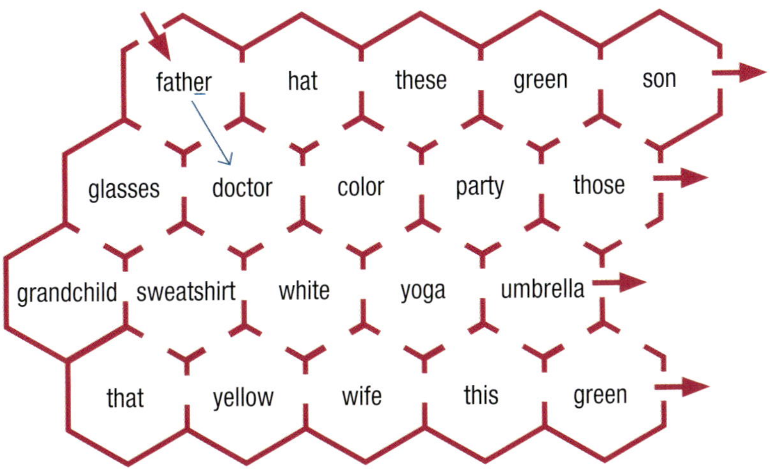

GRAMMAR
have/has

A WORK IT OUT Read the phrases from *100 years young!* Underline examples of *have/has*. Then choose the correct option to complete the rule.

Lilly has two children, …
'I don't have a son or a grandson, …'
'Do you have any men in your family?'
'Yes, I do, …' I have a husband, …'

have/has
We use *have/has* to talk about *somebody's age* / *family members and things that we own*.

B WORK IT OUT Complete the table with the words in the box.

do doesn't doesn't have don't have has ~~have (x3)~~

have/has	
positive (+)	I [1] ___have___ a sister She [2] ________ a brother.
negative (–)	I [3] ________ a brother. He [4] ________ a granddaughter.
question	Do you [5] ________ a daughter? Does she [6] ________ a daughter?
answer	Yes, I [7] ________. / No, I don't. Yes, she does / No, he [8] ________.

C Go to the Grammar Hub on page 102.

SPEAKING HUB

A PREPARE Draw your family tree on a piece of paper and write the family members. Don't write their names and don't write your name.

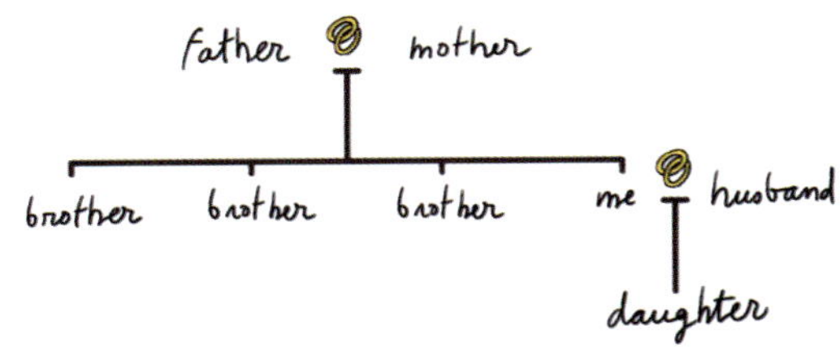

B DISCUSS Work in groups. Follow the instructions:

- Fold your family trees and put them in a box.
- Take out another person's family tree.
- Ask and answer questions. Find out who each family tree belongs to.

A: Do you have a sister, Nita?
B: No, I don't.
A: Do you have three brothers?
B: Yes, I do.
A: Is this your family tree?
B: Yes, it is!

C PRACTICE Ask each other more questions about the people in your families.

A: What's your brother's name?
B: His name's Hector.
A: How old is he?
B: He's 34.
A: What does he do?
B: He's a builder.

Talk about your family

Café Hub

3.3 Guess who

F – describe people

COMPREHENSION

A Watch the video. Number the events (a–d) in the order you see them (1–4). Is it easy for Gaby to meet Lucy?

a ____

b ____

c ____

d ____

B Are the sentences true (T) or false (F)? Watch the video again and check your answers.

1 Gaby sees Lucy's poster in Sam's Café. T / F
2 Gaby texts Lucy first. T / F
3 Lucy has a yellow jacket. T / F
4 Lucy is English. T / F
5 Lucy has a green scarf. T / F
6 At Sam's Café, all the women have green jackets. T / F
7 Gaby says she's not OK. T / F
8 Gaby is Lucy's new Spanish teacher. T / F

C Correct the false sentences in Exercise B.

D How many bags, chairs, etc can you see in the picture?

bags	*3*	laptops	____	men	____	tables	____
chairs	____	plants	____	people	____	women	____

GABY

SAM

LUCY

FUNCTIONAL LANGUAGE

Describing people

Subject + verb	Type	Color	Noun
I've got	long	brown	hair.
I have	light	brown	hair.
Gaby's got a		yellow	jacket.

A Put the words in 1–5 in the correct order. Use the box to help you.

1 got / a / jacket. / green / She's

____

2 got / They've all / jackets. / green

____

3 Lucy's / hair. / brown / light / got

____

4 got / Lucy's / bag. / black / a

____

5 gray / got / Lucy's / a / scarf.

____

B 01:39–02:20 Watch part of the video and check your answers to Exercise A.

C Complete the descriptions with the words in the box.

blond curly long straight

1 short __________ hair

2 __________ red hair

3 __________ gray hair

4 __________ black hair

D **SPEAK** Work in pairs. Play a game of *Guess who* in the class.

A: She has long brown hair.
B: Is it Sandra?
A: Yes it is.

PRONUNCIATION

3.7 **A** Listen to the conversation. Notice how the underlined words are stressed.

Jessica: Hi, Mark. Are you free at two o'clock?
Mark: Yes!
Jessica: Do you know Sam's Café?
Mark: Yes. See you there at two o'clock. I have light brown hair and a black coat.
Jessica: OK. I have long black hair, a green coat and a yellow scarf.

3.7 **B** Listen again and repeat the conversation. Copy the stress.

C **SPEAK** Work in pairs. Practice the conversation.

SPEAKING

A **PLAN** Work in pairs. You want to do a language exchange. Arrange to meet your partner – you don't know each other.

- Choose a time and a place to meet.
- Write notes about your appearance.

B **PRACTICE** Work in pairs. Write and practice a similar conversation to the one in Pronunciation Exercise A.

C **REPEAT** Swap roles. Choose a new time and place to meet.

Note

I've got **(British)** = I have **(American)**
She's got **(British)** = She has **(American)**

The word *got* is typically not used with *has* and *have* in standard American English.

Describe people

3 Writing — Write a social media post

W– using *but*

A Read the social media post. Whose birthday is it today? Match the picture with the event.

Florence Duprey
January 24, 9:21 am

Happy birthday to my sister Martina! Here we are at home. She's wearing the yellow sweater and has a big smile – she's one in this picture! Our mom took this photo. Today it's Martina's 30th birthday party! We have the cake, but Mom is late 😊! Our little sister Talia is here, too – she's in the yellow top next to her husband Larry. Martina has a husband, too. His name is Paulo – he's the one in the white sweater.

5   20   9

Using *but*

We use *but* to join ideas that are different.

We have the cake, **but** *mom is late!*

B Read the post again. These sentences are all false. Correct the sentences.

1 Martina is two years old in the first picture.

______________________________.

2 Martina's mom is at Martina's 30th birthday party.

______________________________.

3 Martina has one sister.

______________________________.

4 Larry is wearing a white sweater.

______________________________.

WRITING

A PLAN You are going to write a social media post. Find a picture of people in your family on a special day. Plan what you want to say.

B WRITE Write a social media post for the picture.

Write a social media post

Unit 3 Review

GRAMMAR

A Complete the sentences with *this, that, these* or *those*.

1 ________ bag is red.
2 ________ bag is blue.

3 ________ bags are red.
4 ________ bags are blue.

B Complete the sentences with *is* or *are*.

1 This bag ___*is*___ green.
2 Those hats ________ yellow.
3 Those headphones ________ black.
4 These glasses ________ white.
5 This phone ________ gray.
6 Those bags ________ brown.

C Choose the correct option to complete the sentences.

1 *I have/ has* a son.
2 *Do you has / Do you have* a brown coat? Yes, I *do/does.*
3 I *don't have / doesn't have* a brother.
4 She *don't have / doesn't have* a granddaughter.
5 *Does / Do* he have a brother? No, he *don't / doesn't.*

VOCABULARY

A Complete the words for objects and colors.

1 My h _e_ _a_ _d_ p _h_ _o_ _n_ _e_ _s_ are g _r_ _e_ _e_ _n_.
2 This u __ b ___ ___ ___ l __ is w ___ ___ ___ ___.
3 I have a b ___ ___ ___ n s w ___ ___ ___ s h ___ ___ ___.
4 My g l ___ ___ ___ ___ ___ are g ___ ___ ___.
5 That is a b __ u __ c o __ t.
6 These are my __ l __ c k b __ g s.

B Use the information. Write the names of the people.

Angela is 6. Mary is 35. Cara is 70.

1 ___*Cara*___: 'Mary is my daughter.'
2 ________: 'Cara is my grandmother.'
3 ________: 'Angela is my daughter.'

Pietro is 10. Guillermo is 50. Giancarlo is 80.

4 ________: 'Pietro is my grandson.'
5 ________: 'Giancarlo is my father.'
6 ________: 'Guillermo is my father.'

4 TIME

Better three hours too soon than a minute too late.
William Shakespeare

Sunset over Alhambra Palace, Granada, Spain.

OBJECTIVES

- talk about daily routines
- talk about annual routines
- order in a café
- write an email about your routine

Work with a partner. Discuss the questions.

1 Look at the picture. Which words match the picture?

city countryside moon morning night ocean sky sun

2 What's your favorite time of day?

3 Read the quote. Are you usually early or late for things?

4.1 Every day

Talk about daily routines

V daily activities; time **G** simple present: *I, you, we, they* **P** sentence stress

VOCABULARY

Daily activities

A Match the sentences (1–4) with the pictures (a–d).

1 I finish work at six ten in the evening.
2 I get up at seven o'clock in the morning.
3 I go to work at eight thirty in the morning.
4 I get home at five o'clock in the afternoon.

B Go to the Vocabulary Hub on page 123.

Time

4.1 Complete the times with the numbers in the box. Then listen and check.

eight eleven fifty forty-five nine twelve

1

_______ o'clock

2

_______ ten

3

twelve _______

4

_______ thirty

5

_______ fifteen

6

one _______

LISTENING

A PREPARE TO LISTEN Read the information about the podcast. Then choose the correct options to complete the summary.

The title of this podcast series is *My life*. In this episode, [1]*three / two* people talk about [2]*the people they know / the things they do*. The people in this episode have the same [3]*hobby / job*.

4.2 **B** LISTEN FOR MAIN IDEA Listen to the podcast and choose the correct options to complete the sentences.

1 Magne is Astrid's …
 a brother. b husband.
2 Astrid and Magne live and work … .
 a in the same place. b in different places.
3 Astrid and Magne work …
 a at the same time. b at different times.

4.2 **C** LISTEN FOR DETAIL Listen again. Circle the correct person: Astrid (A) or Magne (M).

1 1 am go to bed A / M
2 5 am get up A / M
3 5:15 am start work A / M
4 11 am get up A / M
5 1:30 pm start work A / M
6 1:30 pm finish work A / M
7 8 pm go to bed A / M
8 9:45 pm finish work A / M

D DISCUSS Work in pairs. Which person's day do you prefer? Why?

GRAMMAR

Simple present: *I, you, we, they*

A Read the sentences from the podcast. Are they positive (+) or negative (–)?

a I get up at five o'clock in the morning. + / –

b I don't work in the morning. + / –

B **WORK IT OUT** Complete the table with the words in the box.

don't go go

Simple present: *I, you, we, they*			
subject pronoun	positive	subject pronoun	negative
I you we they	[1] ______ to work at eight o'clock in the morning.	I you we they	[2] ______ to work at six o'clock in the morning.

C **WORK IT OUT** Read the sentences again. Choose the correct option to complete the rules.

1 In positive sentences with *I, you, we*, and *they* we use *verb / do + verb*.

2 In negative sentences with *I, you, we*, and *they* we use *verb / don't + verb*.

D Go to the **Grammar Hub** on **page 104**.

E **PRACTICE** Complete the description with the correct positive or negative form of the verbs in the box.

finish get up (x2) go start ~~work~~

The night shift

I'm a doctor. For one week in each month, I [1] *don't work* during the day. I [2] ______ my job at ten o'clock in the evening and I [3] ______ at eight o'clock in the morning. I [4] ______ in the morning, like most people. I [5] ______ in the evening, and I [6] ______ to bed in the morning.

F **SPEAK** Work in pairs. What times do you think these people get up and go to bed?

5-year-old children 80-year-old people

20-year-old people People your age

PRONUNCIATION

Sentence stress

A Listen and repeat the sentences. Which words are stressed – the red or the blue? 4.3

1 I go to bed at ten o'clock.

2 I don't go to bed at ten o'clock.

B Underline the stressed words in the sentences. Then listen and check. 4.4

1 I read a book in the evening.

2 We don't watch TV in the morning.

3 They start work at eight o'clock in the morning.

4 They don't start at eight thirty.

5 I relax in the evening.

C Listen and complete the sentences. 4.5

1 I ______ to ______ at ______ o'clock.

2 I ______ ______ in the ______.

3 They ______ ______ to ______ at ______ thirty.

4 We ______ ______ in the ______.

SPEAKING

A **PREPARE** Think about these daily activities. Check (✓) the ones that you do every day.

- ☐ get up
- ☐ have breakfast
- ☐ go to work/school
- ☐ start work/classes
- ☐ have lunch
- ☐ finish work/classes
- ☐ go home
- ☐ have dinner
- ☐ watch TV/a movie
- ☐ read a book
- ☐ talk to friends/family
- ☐ go to bed

B **PLAN** Write the times you do the things in Exercise A. Prepare how to say it.

C **DISCUSS** Work in pairs. Compare your daily routines. What's different? What's the same?

A: I get up at seven o'clock in the morning.

B: I get up at eight o'clock in the morning.

Talk about daily routines

4.2 Every year

Talk about annual routines

V – months and seasons
G – simple present questions: *I, you, we, they*
S – using pictures before you read
P – *do you* /ʤʊ/

a

b

c

d

VOCABULARY
Months and seasons

A Match the pictures with the seasons.

fall   spring   summer   winter

4.6 **B** Listen and complete the calendar.

April   August   December   July   June   March
May   November   October   September

January	February	

C SPEAK Work in pairs. Answer the questions.

- Which season is it now?
- Which month is it now?
- Which season is your favorite?
- Which month is your birthday in?

READING

A PREDICT Work in pairs. Look at the pictures in the article *Nomads in Mongolia* but don't read the text. What do you know about these people's lives?

Using pictures before you read

Articles on websites and in magazines and newspapers usually have pictures. Look at the pictures before you read to get an idea of what the text is about.

B PREPARE TO READ Match the words in the box with the pictures (a–d) in *Nomads in Mongolia* opposite.

hills   horse   river   tents

C READ FOR GIST Read the article. Match the correct question (a–d) with each paragraph (1–4).

a How often do they go to a different place?
b What are nomads?
c Where do they go in different seasons?
d Do they live in houses?

D READ FOR DETAIL Read the article again. Are the statements true (T) or false (F)?

1 Mongolia is in Europe. T / F
2 Nomads live in cities. T / F
3 Nomads live in a type of tent. T / F
4 Nomads have animals. T / F
5 In Mongolia, September is in the spring. T / F
6 Many nomads go to a river in the spring. T / F

E SPEAK Work in pairs. Answer the questions.

- Are there nomads in your country?
- Would you like to live in different places in your country at different times of the year?

NOMADS
in Mongolia

Mongolia is a large country in Asia, north of China and south of Russia. There's a lot of space, about 1.56 million km², but there aren't a lot of people. There are about 3,000,000 (three million) people in Mongolia and many of these people are nomads.

1 ____ Nomads are people who go to different places in different months or seasons. They don't live in cities, they live in the countryside.

2 ____ No, they don't. They don't have houses, but they have tents, called *gers*, and they have horses and other animals.

3 ____ Some nomads move thirty times a year, some move four times a year. Many nomads go to a different place in the spring and in the fall. In Mongolia, spring is March, April and May, and fall is September and October.

4 ____ In the spring, they go close to a river for water. In the fall, they go to the hills.

GRAMMAR
Simple present questions: *I, you, we, they*

A Read two of the questions from *Nomads in Mongolia*. Match the questions (a and b) with the correct question type (1 and 2).

a Where do they go? b Do they live in houses?

1 Question ___ is a *yes/no* question. The answer can be *yes* or *no*.
2 Question ___ is a *wh-* question. The answer depends on the question word.

B WORK IT OUT Read the questions again and find their answers in the text. Complete the rules.

Simple present questions: *I, you, we, they*

1 In *yes/no* questions we use *do* **before / after** *I, you, we,* and *they*.
2 In *wh-* questions we use a question word (for example *what, where, when …*) **before / after** *do*.
3 To give short answers to *yes/no* questions we **use *do* or *don't* / repeat the main verb**.

C Go to the **Grammar Hub** on **page 104**.

D PRACTICE Reorder the words to make questions. Choose the correct question type.

1 go to work / you / when / in the morning / do
When do you go to work in the morning?
a *yes/no* b (*wh-*)
2 you / go / to another country / in the summer / do
_______________?
a *yes/no* b *wh-*
3 talk to / in the evening / you / do / who
_______________?
a *yes/no* b *wh-*
4 in the same place / live / you / do / all year
_______________?
a *yes/no* b *wh-*

E SPEAK Work in pairs. Ask and answer the questions in Exercise D.

a

b

c

d

PRONUNCIATION
Do you /dʒʊ/

A 4.7 Read and listen to the questions. How does the speaker say the underlined words?

1 Do you live in the countryside?
2 When do you go to work?

B 4.8 Work in pairs. Say these questions. Then listen and repeat.

1 Do you get home at seven thirty?
2 Where do you live?
3 Do you read a book in the evening?
4 What do you do in the summer?

C SPEAK Work in pairs. Ask and answer the questions in Exercises A and B.

A: Do you live in the countryside?
B: No, I don't. I live in the city.

SPEAKING HUB

A PREPARE Work in pairs. Student A – Use the information below. Student B – Go to the **Communication Hub** on **page 131**.

Student A – Write questions to find out information about the birds in the picture above.

1 what / called _______________?
2 where / live _______________?
3 where / go / August or September _______________?
4 where / go / May or June _______________?
5 how far / go *How far do they go every year*?

B DISCUSS Ask your partner the questions in Exercise A. Complete the missing information.

C DISCUSS Read the information about gray whales. Answer your partner's questions.

Name: Gray whales
Where: Near Alaska and near Mexico.
When: In the fall (October, November, December) they go to Alaska. In the spring (February, March, April) they go to Mexico.
How far: About 10,000–12,000 miles per year (16,000–20,000 kilometers)

Talk about annual routines

Café Hub

4.3 Coffee chaos

F– order in a café

COMPREHENSION

A Watch the video without sound. Underline the correct word or phrase.

1 The first customer *is* / *isn't* sure what she wants.
2 Sam *is* / *isn't* sure what the customer wants.
3 The line *is* / *isn't* long behind her.
4 The other customers are *fast* / *slow*.
5 Sam *is* / *isn't* happy to see the customer again.

B Read the list of things you can buy in Sam's Café. Watch the video again. Check (✓) the things you hear.

coffee	☐	water	☐
latte	☐	soya milk	☐
cappuccino	☐	bread	☐
mocha	☐	croissants	☐
hot chocolate	☐	snacks	☐
tea	☐	soft drinks	☐

C Use a word from each column to describe the coffee the woman buys.

a small a medium a large	soya	cappuccino latte	to drink in to take away

D Who says it? Sam, the woman or the man in the line? Watch the video again and check your answers.

1 What type of coffee would you like? ____________
2 That's a great question! ____________
3 Come on! ____________
4 What kind of bread do you have? ____________
5 Medium! I mean medium. ____________
6 So, let me check. ____________
7 No problem. ____________
8 How big is a medium? ____________

E SPEAK Work in pairs. What do you think the phrase 'Come on!' means in this context?

Glossary

soya milk **(n) (British)** = soy milk **(n) (American)**
take away **(phrsal v) (British)** = take out or to go **(phrsal v) (American)**

GABY

SAM

LUCY

FUNCTIONAL LANGUAGE

Ordering in a café

A Complete the phrases with the words in the box. Then complete the headings with *Customer* or *Sam*.

Can check get have kind large One please Sorry want What you

A ______	B ______
What can I [1] ______ you?	[7] ______ I have a latte / a soya latte / a tea / a hot chocolate, please?
[2] ______ type of coffee would you like?	Do [8] ______ have soya milk?
Sure. Small, medium or [3] ______?	Can I [9] ______ a small, please?
So, let me [4] ______: you [5] ______ a medium soya latte to take away?	A soya latte, please.
[6] ______, we're closing now.	[10] ______ tea / hot chocolate, please.
	Two cappuccinos, [11] ______.
	What [12] ______ of bread do you have?

B Watch the video again and check your answers to Exercise A.

PRONUNCIATION

4.9 **A** Listen to the conversation. Notice how the underlined words are stressed.

Coffee seller: Good morning! What can I get you?
Customer: Can I have a coffee, please?
Coffee seller: What type of coffee would you like?
Customer: A cappuccino, please. Do you have soy milk?
Coffee seller: Sure. One soy cappuccino. Small, medium or large?
Customer: Can I have a medium, please? To go.
Coffee seller: So, you want a medium, soy cappuccino to go?
Customer: Yes, please.

4.9 **B** Listen again and repeat the conversation. Copy the stress.

C SPEAK Work in pairs. Practice the conversation.

SPEAKING

Coffee	small	medium	large
Latte	$2.00	$2.50	$3.00
Cappuccino	$2.00	$2.50	$3.00
Americano	$1.70	$2.20	$2.70
Mocha	$2.00	$2.50	$3.00
Hot chocolate	$2.00	$2.50	$3.00
Tea	$1.00	$1.50	$2.00

Croissant $2.00 Bread and jam $2.50

A PREPARE Work in pairs. Take turns being Student A and B. Replace the underlined words. Use the menu to help you.

Student A: What can I get you?
Student B: Can I have a cappuccino, please?
Student A: Small, medium or large?
Student B: Can I have a small, please?
Student A: Sure. One small cappuccino.
Student B: Thanks.

B PRACTICE Have a new conversation. Student A works in a café. Student B is a difficult customer. Practice your conversation.

C PRESENT Show your conversation to the class. Who is the best difficult customer?

Order in a café

4 Writing

Write an email about your routine

W using contractions

A Read the email from Hadid to his friend Javier. Where does Hadid work?

To: Javier
From: Hadid
How are you?

Hi Javier,

How are you? I don't work in Madrid anymore. I work on an oil rig. It's in the middle of the ocean. I work here every spring. I get to the oil rig in March, and I go home in April.

We get up at six o'clock in the morning, and we start work at seven. We finish work at seven o'clock in the evening – it's a long day! I don't have time to read a book or watch TV in the evening. I eat, talk to my family on the phone and go to bed at nine o'clock.

What about you? Where are you now? What's your job?

See you,

Hadid

Using contractions

When we write to friends or family, we can use contractions:

I'm for *I am*

it's for *it is*.

B Read the email again. Match the activities (1–6) with the months and times (a–f).

1	get to the oil rig	**a**	7 am
2	go home	**b**	7 pm
3	get up	**c**	March
4	start work	**d**	April
5	finish work	**e**	9 pm
6	go to bed	**f**	6 am

C SPEAK Work in pairs. Answer the question.

Do you think Hadid's routine is good? Why/Why not?

WRITING

A PLAN You are going to write an email to an old friend. Write notes about your daily routine.

B WRITE Write your email. Tell them about your daily routine. Use contractions.

Write an email about your routine

Unit 4 Review

GRAMMAR

Put the words in the correct order to make sentences.

1 do / get up / you / what time
What time do you get up ?

2 live / in Spain / they
________________.

3 watch / TV in the evening / you / don't
________________.

4 like / soccer / don't / we
________________.

5 you / start work / when / do
________________?

6 they / do / why / at five o'clock / get up
________________?

VOCABULARY

A Complete the sentences with the words in the box.

get get up go (x2) finish watch

1 I ________ at six o'clock in the morning.
2 I ________ to work at eight thirty in the morning.
3 I ________ work at five thirty in the afternoon.
4 I ________ home at six ten.
5 I relax and ________ TV at seven thirty in the evening.
6 I ________ to bed at ten forty-five at night.

B Match the sentences in Exercise A with these times.

a 5:30 pm ___ **c** 6:10 pm ___ **e** 8:30 am ___
b 6 am ___ **d** 10:45 pm ___ **f** 7:30 pm ___

C Complete the words in these sentences.

1 My birthday is in F _ _ _ _ _ _ _.
2 My favorite season is _ _ _ t _ _.
3 _ _ _ is the month after April.
4 In my country, the _ _ m _ _ _ is June, July and A _ _ _ _ _.

5 TIME FOR A BREAK

Guard well your spare moments.

Ralph Waldo Emerson

Two men sitting on metal drums, Perth, Australia.

OBJECTIVES

- talk about free time
- talk about food and meals
- ask for information
- write a blog about food

Work with a partner. Discuss the questions.

1 Look at the picture. Why are these people happy?
2 What's your favorite food?
3 What makes you feel happy?

5.1 Relax and be happy

Talk about free time

V free-time activities G simple present: *he, she, it* P *does he / does she*

VOCABULARY

Free-time activities

A Look at the pictures. What is the same about all these activities?

1 ______ for a walk

2 ______ in the backyard

3 ______ a meal

4 ______ a bath

5 ______ shopping

6 ______ chess

7 ______ to the gym

8 ______ running

5.1 **B** Match the verbs with the pictures. Listen and check.

cook go (x4) take play sit

C SPEAK Work in pairs. What do you do to relax?

LISTENING

5.2 **A LISTEN FOR GIST** Listen to an interview. Which of the free-time activities from Vocabulary Exercise A do the people talk about?

5.2 **B LISTEN FOR DETAIL** Listen again. Are these sentences true (T) or false (F)?

1 The man eats lunch in his office. *T / F*
2 The woman goes to the gym on her lunch break. *T / F*
3 The woman goes for a walk after work. *T / F*
4 The woman watches TV in the evening. *T / F*
5 The man goes running after work. *T / F*
6 The woman goes running on the weekend. *T / F*

GRAMMAR

Simple present: *he, she, it*

A Read the examples. <u>Underline</u> the verbs.

He works all the time! He doesn't even take coffee breaks.

Does she go to the gym every day?

No, she doesn't. She goes about twice a week.

She doesn't have time to relax!

B WORK IT OUT Complete the rules with words in the box.

does doesn't main verb question word without

Simple present: *he, she, it*

1 In positive sentences, we use the ______________ plus *-s* or *-es*.
2 In negative sentences, we use ______________ plus the main verb without *-s*.
3 In *yes/no* questions, we use *Does* followed by the subject and the main verb ______________ *-s*.
4 In short answers, we use ______________ or *doesn't*.
5 In *wh-* questions, we use a ______________ and *does* plus the main verb without *-s*.

C PRACTICE Choose the correct option to complete the sentences.

1 Martin *cook* / *cooks* dinner in the evening.
2 Anna *don't* / *doesn't* go shopping after work.
3 Does Paolo *play* / *plays* chess?
4 What does Shyama *do* / *does* on the weekend?
5 **A:** Does Akira *takes* / *take* a bath after work?
B: Yes, he *takes* / *does*.

D Go to the **Grammar Hub** on **page 106**.

E PRACTICE Complete the conversation.

Anna: What do you [1] ______________ to relax on the weekend? Do you go shopping?

Bea: No, I don't. My husband [2] ______________ shopping, and I [3] ______________ running. What about you?

Anna: I [4] ______________ to the gym and my husband [5] ______________ TV and [6] ______________ computer games.

Bea: That sounds good. What kind of games [7] ______________ he play?

Anna: He [8] ______________ action games.

PRONUNCIATION

does he / does she

A 5.3 Read and listen to the questions. Notice how the speaker links the <u>underlined</u> words together.

1 <u>Does he</u> go the gym?
2 <u>Does she</u> go running?

B 5.4 Listen to each question and circle the words you hear.

1 *Does he* / *Does she* cook dinner every night?
2 *Does he* / *Does she* go shopping on the weekend?
3 What *does he* / *does she* do at lunchtime?
4 What kind of food *does he* / *does she* cook?

C 5.4 Listen and repeat the questions in Exercise B.

SPEAKING

A PREPARE Complete the table with your free-time activities. Write three activities in each box.

	Me	My partner
On your lunch break		
In the evening		
On the weekend		

B DISCUSS Work in pairs. Ask your partner questions to complete the table. How many things are the same for both of you?

What do you do on your lunch break? Do you go for a walk?

C REPORT Tell the class about your partner.

Anton goes shopping on the weekend. He doesn't cook meals at home.

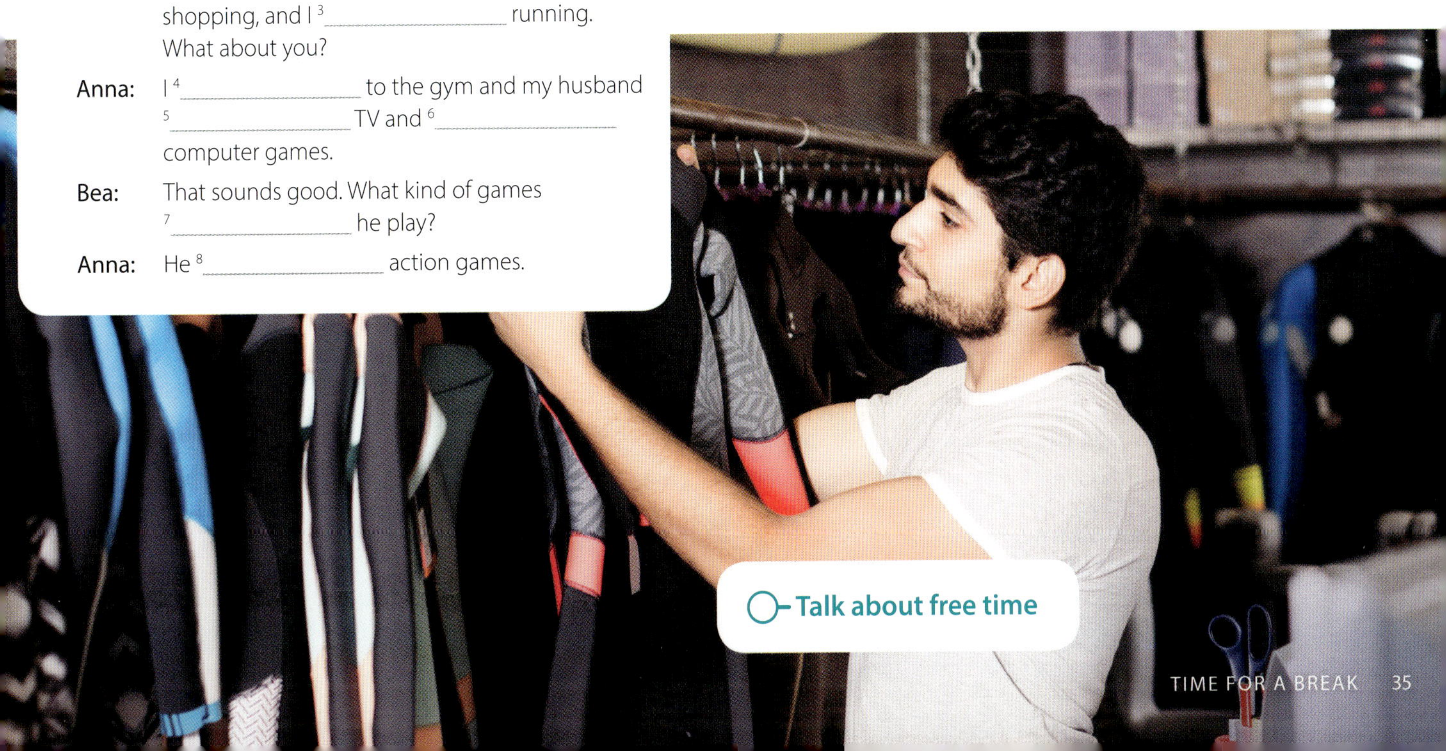

Talk about free time

5.2 When's your lunch break?

Talk about food and meals

V food and meals **S** skimming **G** adverbs of frequency **P** linking with /j/

VOCABULARY

Food and meals

A Look at the pictures. Which food do you eat for breakfast, lunch or dinner?

a  ______

b  ______

c  ______

d  ______

e  ______

f  ______

g  ______

h  ______

i  ______

j  ______

k  ______

l  ______

B Match the words in the box to the pictures.

apples	beans	bread	cereal	cheese	chicken
eggs	fish	noodles	pasta	potatoes	rice

C Go to the **Vocabulary Hub** on **page 124**.

D **SPEAK** Make a list of food you eat every day. Tell your partner. What's the same? What's different?

READING

A **PREPARE** Work in pairs. Look at the pictures. Which foods can you name? Where do you think they come from?

 ______

 ______

 ______

Skimming

When you skim a text, you read it quickly to get the general idea.

B **SKIM** Read *Lunch breaks around the world* and match the correct people with the pictures in Exercise A.

C **READ FOR GIST** Read the article. Which questions do all three people answer? Check (✓) the questions.

- **a** What do you eat for lunch? ☐
- **b** Is your lunch expensive? ☐
- **c** What time is your lunch break? ☐
- **d** Who do you eat lunch with? ☐
- **e** Where do you eat lunch? ☐
- **f** Do you eat a big lunch? ☐

D **READ FOR DETAIL** Read the article again. Write the correct names.

1 ______ eats soup for lunch.
2 ______ doesn't eat rice for lunch.
3 ______ eats lunch at work.
4 ______ doesn't talk about a drink.
5 ______ has lunch with family.
6 ______ has more than an hour for lunch.

LUNCH BREAKS AROUND THE WORLD

More and more people in the US don't take a lunch break. They eat lunch at their desk instead. Here we take a look at countries around the world and what workers do on their lunch breaks.

Sara, Japan

We always take our lunch break at the same time every day, from 12 to 1. Some people bring a lunchbox from home, but I always go to the office cafeteria to eat with my colleagues. The food is usually really good. I usually have rice with fish or chicken and some vegetables. After lunch, I have a cup of green tea. I drink a lot of green tea every day because it's good for my health.

Davide, Italy

Our lunch break is from 1:30 to 2:30. Sometimes we go to a local restaurant for lunch, but I usually go home. My wife always comes home for lunch, and we eat together. We usually have a small dish of pasta. After that we have some freshly cooked meat or fish. My favorite is chicken in tomato sauce. For dessert, we always have some fruit and finally a cup of coffee.

GRAMMAR
Adverbs of frequency

A Find and complete the sentences with adverbs from *Lunch breaks around the world*.

1 The food is ________________ really good.
2 I ________________ have rice with fish or chicken and some vegetables.
3 ________________ we go to a local restaurant for lunch.
4 My wife ________________ comes home for lunch.
5 I ________________ have dessert.
6 I ________________ have some fruit or something sweet as a special treat.

B Complete the chart with *sometimes*, *usually* and *never*.

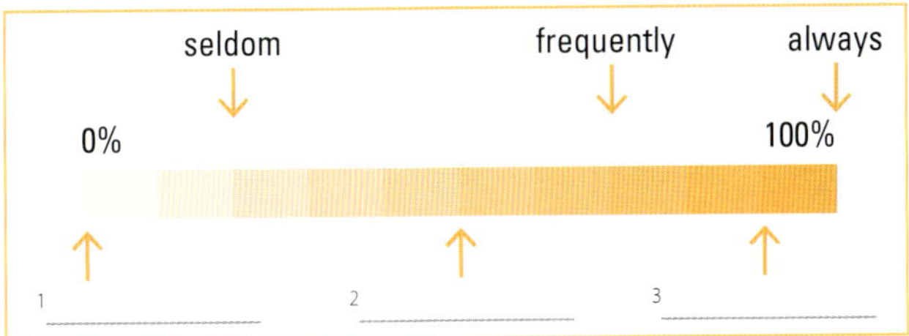

C **WORK IT OUT** Read the sentences in Exercise A and choose the correct option to complete the rules.

Adverbs of frequency

We use adverbs of frequency to say how often we do things. We put them …

1 *before / after* the verb *be* (in positive and negative sentences).
2 *before / after* other verbs (in positive sentences).

D Go to the **Grammar Hub** on **page 106**.

E **SPEAK** Work in pairs. How often do you eat these kinds of food? When do you eat them? Tell your partner.

bread cheese chocolate coffee
fish fruit ice cream milk rice tea

A: I usually have coffee for breakfast.
B: I frequently have coffee, but I sometimes have tea.

Natalia, Guatemala

Lunch is the main meal in Guatemala. I usually take a lunch break from 12 to 1:30 and have lunch with my friends or colleagues in a restaurant near the office. We usually have some soup and tortillas with rice and beans, some meat and a salad. I never have dessert, but later in the day, I frequently have some fruit or something sweet as a special treat.

PRONUNCIATION
Linking with /j/

5.5 **A** Listen to the sentence. Notice how the /j/ sound links the words joined with a ‿.

She‿always eats lunch at work.

5.6 **B** Read and listen. Draw a ‿ to show the words linked with a /j/ sound.

1 He always drinks coffee.
2 I usually have a salad.
3 She eats pasta for lunch.
4 We all eat fish and rice.

5.6 **C** Listen again and repeat the examples.

SPEAKING HUB

A **PREPARE** You are going to take a survey of eating habits in your class. Complete the questions (1–6).

EATING HABITS SURVEY

1 Do you *usually drink coffee for breakfast*?
a ________________ usually drinks coffee for breakfast.
2 Do you ________________?
b ________________ always cooks dinner at home.
3 Do you ________________?
c ________________ frequently eats lunch at work.
4 Do you ________________?
d ________________ sometimes eats pizza for lunch.
5 Do you ________________?
e ________________ never eats chocolate.
6 Do you ________________?
f ________________ seldom eats meat.

B **PRACTICE** Ask your classmates the survey questions. Write names in sentences a–f. Ask each person another question to get more information.

A: Do you usually drink coffee for breakfast?
B: No, I don't.
A: What do you usually drink for breakfast?
B: I usually drink tea or hot chocolate.

C **REPORT** Tell the class about your answers.

Jerome doesn't drink coffee for breakfast. He usually drinks tea or hot chocolate.

Talk about food and meals

Café Hub

5.3 No battery

F – ask for information

COMPREHENSION

A ▶ Watch the video. Complete the information about the train ticket.

2 3 85 afternoon return

1 Gaby wants a ticket to Manchester on Saturday ________.
2 It leaves at ________ pm.
3 It takes about ________ hours.
4 She wants a ________ ticket.
5 It costs £ ________.

B ▶ Watch the video again and put the events (a–f) in the correct order (1–6).

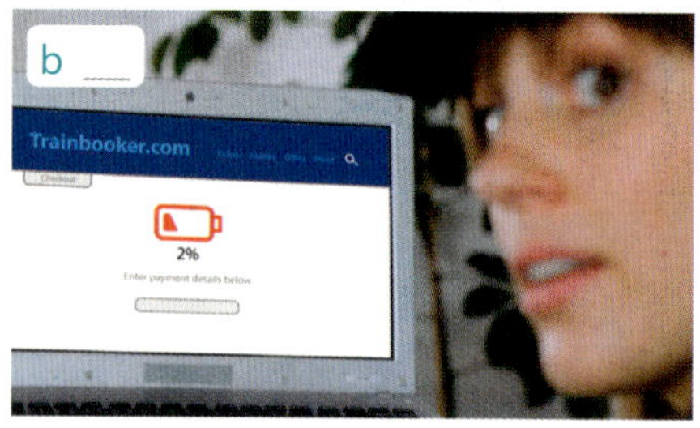

C ▶ Match the phrases (1–6) with the pictures (a–f) in Exercise B. Then watch the video again and check your answers.

1 It worked! ___
2 Gaby hates computers. d
3 Lucy needs Gaby's credit card. ___
4 There's no battery. ___
5 Lucy has an idea. ___
6 The wi-fi stops working. ___

USEFUL PHRASES

A Complete the useful phrases with the words in the box.

expensive idea matter news see worked

1 I have an ________!
2 Let me ________.
3 Good ________!
4 What's the ________?
5 Wow, that's ________!
6 It ________!

B ▶ Watch the video again and check your answers to Exercise A.

C **SPEAK** Work in pairs. Complete the conversations with useful phrases from Exercise A. Practice the conversations.

1 A: I don't have a ticket.
B: ________ – I have a ticket for you!
2 A: It's $150.
B: ________!
3 A: What time does it leave?
B: ________.
4 A: Oh no!
B: ________?
5 A: I don't know what to do!
B: ________!
6 A The code doesn't work.
B: Here – try this number.
A: ________!

GABY

SAM

LUCY

FUNCTIONAL LANGUAGE

Asking for information

A Write *Customer* or *Ticket seller* in the correct column, A or B.

A ______	B ______
1 I'd like a ticket to New York on Saturday afternoon.	a That's $85, please.
2 What time does it leave?	b It takes about two hours.
3 How long does it take?	c Saturday afternoon. Yes, there is a train.
4 Can I book a ticket please?	d One-way or round-trip?
5 Round-trip, please.	e It leaves at 3 pm.

B Match the phrases (1–5) with the responses (a–e).

Glossary

pounds **(n) (British)** = dollars **(n) (American)**
return ticket **(n) (British)** = round-trip ticket **(n) (American)**
single ticket **(n) (British)** = one-way ticket **(n) (American)**

PRONUNCIATION

5.7 **A** Listen to the conversation and notice how the underlined words are stressed.

Ticket seller: Can I help you?
Customer: Yes, I'd like a ticket to Boston on Friday morning, please.
Ticket seller: Friday morning. Let me see. Yes, there is a train.
Customer: What time does it leave?
Ticket seller: It leaves at 10:30.
Customer: How long does it take?
Ticket seller: It takes about three hours.
Customer: How much is it?
Ticket seller: Thirty-five dollars.
Customer: Can I book a ticket, please?
Ticket seller: One-way or round-trip?
Customer: One-way, please.

5.7 **B** Listen again and repeat the conversation. Copy the stress.

SPEAKING

DESTINATION	DEPARTURE	ARRIVAL	PRICE	
			one-way	round-trip
Washington, D.C.	10:30	12:30	$30	$55
Baltimore	10:45	11:45	$20	$30
New York City	11:00	1:30	$45	$60
Boston	11:15	3:00	$55	$80

A PREPARE Work in pairs. Complete the conversation using information in the timetable.

I'd like a ticket to ______, please.
There is a train to ______ this morning.
What time ______?
It leaves at ______.
How long ______?
It takes ______.
How much ______?
One-way or ______?
______, please.
That's $______, please.

B PLAN Work in pairs. Add three or more useful phrases to the conversation.

C PRACTICE Work in pairs. Practice the conversation.

D REPEAT Change roles. Choose a new destination.

Ask for information

5 Writing

Write a blog about food

W using object pronouns

A Read Bob's blog. What is the blog post about?

a an everyday lunch
b a special lunch
c how to cook lunch
d Bob's favorite lunch

BOB'S DAILY BLOG

A pot-luck lunch at work

Once a month at work, we have a pot-luck lunch. Everyone cooks some food at home and we bring it to the large meeting room. Some of my colleagues are really good cooks! They bring all kinds of food from their home countries. One of my colleagues is from Mexico and she makes a great chicken dish with chocolate. It's amazing! I'm not a good cook and I usually just bring a salad. We eat and share all the food together – it's a great way to make friends at work!

B Read Bob's blog again. Are these statements true (T) or false (F)?

1 They have a pot-luck lunch every week. *T / F*
2 They eat the pot-luck lunch in a restaurant. *T / F*
3 A colleague makes delicious Mexican food. *T / F*
4 Bob is very good at cooking. *T / F*
5 Bob always brings cupcakes or cookies. *T / F*

Using object pronouns

We use pronouns so we don't need to repeat the noun.

*Everyone cooks some **food** at home and we bring **it** to the large meeting room.*

C Complete the sentences with the correct pronoun.

1 **My brother** works near my office. I meet ______ for lunch every week.
2 We bring different **dishes** to work and share ______ with each other.
3 **My sister** works in Mexico. I visit ______ there every year.
4 I don't go out for **lunch**. I eat ______ at my desk.

WRITING

A PREPARE You are going to write a blog about a special meal tradition in your life. Think about the following points.

- What's special about the meal?
- How often do you have it?
- Where is it?
- What kind of food do you have?
- What's good about this meal?

B WRITE Write your blog.

C REVIEW Read another person's blog. Ask questions to get more information.

Write a blog about food

Unit 5 Review

GRAMMAR

A Choose the correct words to complete the sentences.

1 Sasha *sit* / *sits* in the backyard after work.
2 Eric *doesn't cook* / *cook* dinner during the week.
3 Where does Maria *eat* / *eats* lunch?
4 Does Maha *have* / *has* lunch at school?
5 **A:** *Do* / *Does* Antonio and Sofia eat at home on Friday?
B: No, they *doesn't* / *don't*.
6 **A:** Does Jana *drink* / *drinks* tea every day?
B: Yes, she *do* / *does*.

B Add the adverb to each sentence.

never
1 I am^late for work. (never)
2 We eat breakfast in a café. (sometimes)
3 I cook dinner at home. (frequently)
4 Vicky and Sue have pizza on Friday. (usually)
5 Carey is very busy on the weekend. (always)

VOCABULARY

A Complete the phrases to describe recreational activities.

1 go for a w __ l __
2 take a b __ t __
3 cook a m __ __ l
4 go r __ __ __ __ __ g
5 go to the g __ m
6 play c __ e __ __

B Label the pictures with the correct words.

a

______

b

______

c

______

d

______

e

______

f

______

6 A PLACE TO LIVE

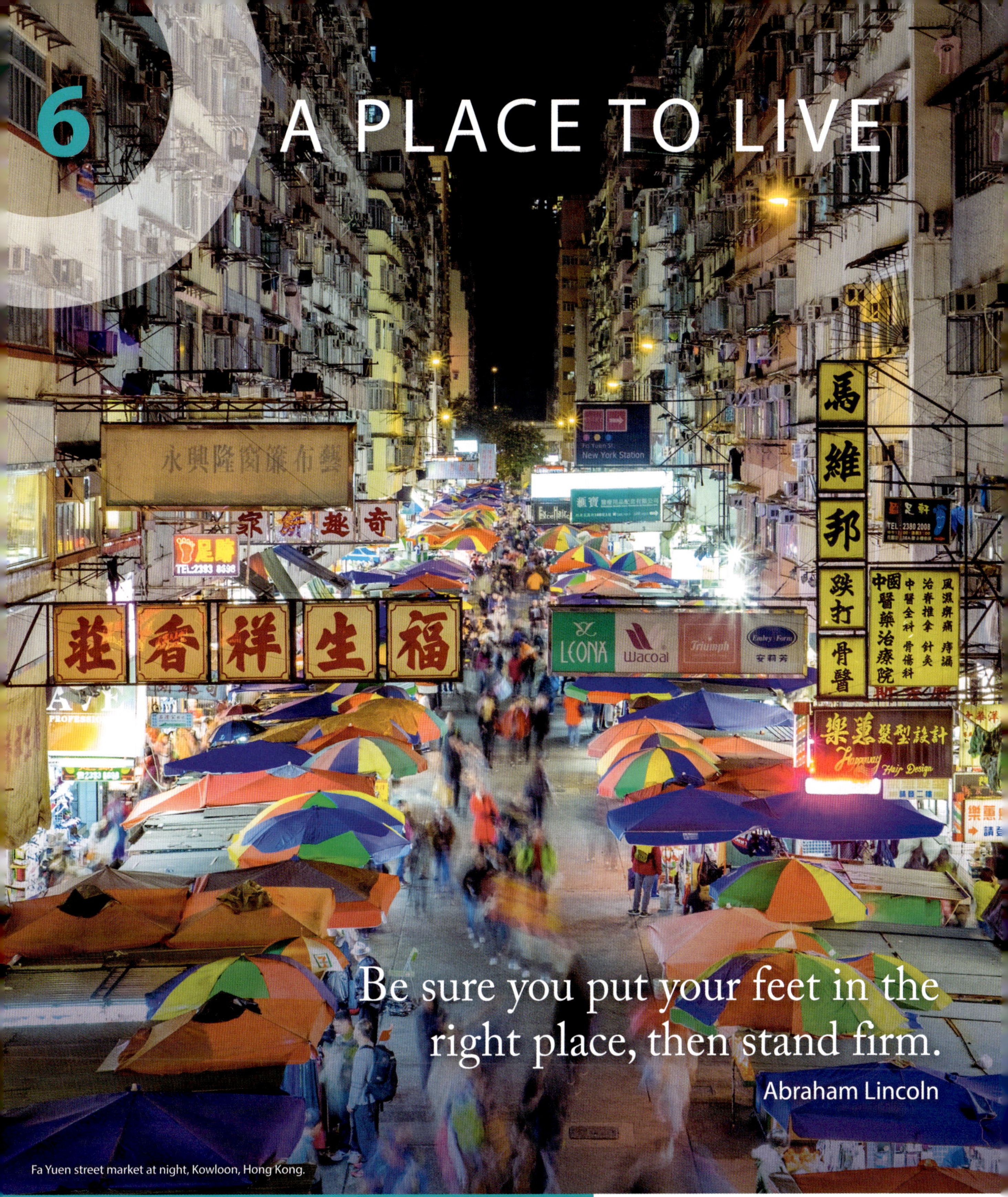

> Be sure you put your feet in the right place, then stand firm.
>
> Abraham Lincoln

Fa Yuen street market at night, Kowloon, Hong Kong.

- describe your town or city
- describe your home
- ask for and give directions
- write a review of a café

Work with a partner. Discuss the questions.

1 Where do you live?

2 Look at the picture. Is this a good place to live? Why/Why not?

3 Complete the sentence in your own words: *Life in a big city is … because …*

cheap dangerous difficult easy expensive horrible nice safe

6.1 Around town

Describe your town or city

V places in a town   **G** *there is / there are; some* and *any*   **P** *there is / there are*

VOCABULARY

Places in a town

6.1 **A** Match the places (1–10) with the words in the box. Then listen and check your answers.

art gallery café hotel market museum park restaurant store station theater

1 ______

2 ______

3 ______

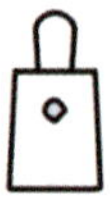
4 ______

5 ______

6 ______

7 ______

8 ______

9 ______

10 ______

6.1 **B** Listen and repeat.

C Complete the sentences with the names of places in a town.

1 I sometimes go to the ______ on the weekend to see a play.
2 We usually buy fresh fruits and vegetables at the ______.
3 Let's visit the ______ to see the paintings.
4 We frequently visit the ______ to learn about history.
5 Let's go out to a ______ for dinner tonight!
6 We frequently stay in a ______ on vacation.
7 I usually take my children to the ______ to play soccer.
8 Let's go to a ______ for some coffee and ice cream!
9 Suzanna frequently goes to the ______ to buy clothes or shoes.
10 How far is it to the ______? My train is at 3 pm.

D SPEAK Work in pairs. Which of these places do you go to in your town?

READING

A PREPARE TO READ Look at the pictures in *What's special about your home town?* Find these things in the pictures.

boat bridge building canal market

B READ FOR GIST Read *What's special about your home town?* Choose the best summary of the main idea.

a Only tourists enjoy Venice.
b Venice is a very difficult place to live.
c Life in Venice is interesting and fun.

C READ FOR GIST Which topics are in the forum post? Check (✓) the answers.

☐ art ☐ food ☐ hotels ☐ jobs ☐ music ☐ schools ☐ transportation

D READ FOR DETAIL Are the sentences true (T) or false (F)?

1 Venice is a modern city. *T / F*
2 Venice is a good city to see art. *T / F*
3 There are hundreds of bridges in Venice. *T / F*
4 There are a lot of cars and buses in the city center. *T / F*
5 The writer takes a water taxi to work. *T / F*

E SPEAK Work in groups. Answer the questions.

1 Is Venice a good place to live, in your opinion? Why/Why not?
2 Is Venice similar to or different from your home town or city?

What's special about
YOUR HOME TOWN?

March 17, 6:57   Reply | Like

I live in Venice, in Italy. It's famous all over the world and there are a lot of tourists. But it's an exciting place to live and work, too.

GRAMMAR

there is / there are; some and *any*

A Read the post again. Underline examples of *there is, there are, some* and *any*.

B **WORK IT OUT** Complete the table using the examples in Exercise A to help you.

there is / there are; some and *any*		
	Singular	Plural
Positive +	There [1] ______ really good café.	There [2] ______ over 400 bridges.
Negative -	There [3] ______ really large grocery store..	There [4] ______ cars.
Some and *a lot of*	We use *some* and *a lot* of with [5]***singular / plural*** nouns. *Some* means a [6]***small / big*** number. *A lot of* means a [7]***small / big*** number. We usually use them in [8]***positive / negative*** sentences.	
Any	We use *any* in [9]***negative / positive*** sentences and in questions.	

C Go to the **Grammar Hub** on **page 108**.

D **SPEAK** Work in pairs. Talk about places near where you are. Use *there is* or *there are* and the words in the box.

art gallery cafés hotel museum restaurants stores

A: There's an art gallery near the school, but there isn't a museum.

B: There are cafés near the school, but there aren't any restaurants.

Venice is a city with a lot of history – I love it! There are some buildings that are over 500 years old! Venice is great for art. There are museums and art galleries everywhere. There are over 400 bridges in Venice. Why? Because there are a lot of canals! There aren't any cars in this area, but there's a train station outside the city center. There aren't any buses in the center either – people go to work by water taxi! There isn't a really large grocery store, but there's a great market with a lot of fresh fruits and vegetables.

I walk to work every morning and look at the buildings and the canals and the bridges. They're amazing! There's a really good café near my home. They make great coffee and fresh sandwiches and I eat breakfast there every morning when I go to work. I think Venice is a great place to live!

PRONUNCIATION

there is / there are

6.2 **A** Read and listen to the examples.

1 There's a restaurant.
2 There's a grocery store.
3 There are some stores.
4 There are some hotels.

6.2 **B** Listen and repeat the sentences in Exercise A.

SPEAKING

A **PLAN** Write the names of places in the chart. Use the words from the Vocabulary section on page 42.

Everyday life	Weekend fun	Food and drink
market		

B **PREPARE** Work in pairs. Are these sentences true or false about your town?

1 There are a lot of parks in my town and there's a museum.
2 There aren't any theaters, but there's an art gallery.
3 There's a large grocery store and there are also a lot of small stores.

C **DISCUSS** Work in groups. Talk about places in your town.

There are a lot of parks in my city. There's a big park near the river and I usually go there with my friends on the weekend.

Describe your town or city

6.2 Choosing a home

Describe your home

V furniture and rooms; prepositions of place
G *is there* / *are there* question forms
S predicting
P vowel sounds: /ʌ/ and /e/

VOCABULARY

Furniture and rooms

A Look at the picture. What kind of person do you think lives here?

B Complete the description with the words in the box.

bed bookshelf chair clock closet cushion desk lamp wall window

The [1] ________ and the [2] ________ are blue. The [3] ________ is green. The [4] ________ is yellow. The [5] ________ is red. The [6] ________ is big. The [7] ________ is brown. The [8] ________ is gray. The [9] ________ is orange. The [10] ________ is light yellow.

6.3 **C** Listen and check your answers to Exercise B .

D Go to the Vocabulary Hub on page 124.

E SPEAK Work in pairs. What furniture do you have in your room at home or your classroom?

Prepositions of place

A Look at the picture in Vocabulary Exercise A again. Complete the description below using *in*, *on* or *under*.

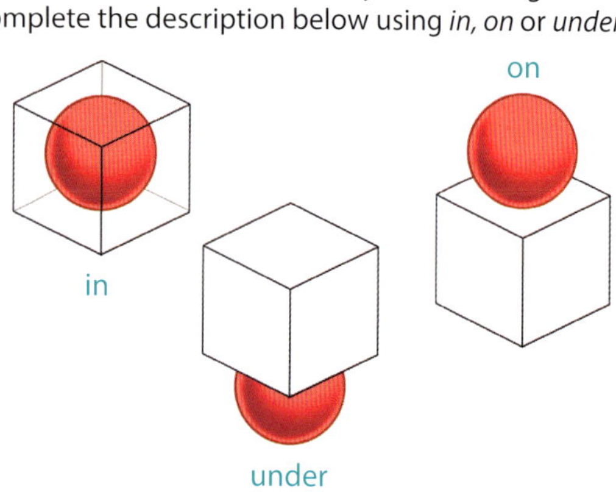

There's a desk and a chair [1] ________ the room. There's a lamp [2] ________ the desk. There are clothes [3] ________ the closet. There are books [4] ________ the bookshelf. There's a small table next to the bed. There's a clock [5] ________ the table. There's a cushion [6] ________ the chair. There's a bag [7] ________ the desk. There's a picture [8] ________ the wall.

6.4 **B** Listen to a description of the room. Find four differences between the picture opposite and the description you hear.

C SPEAK Work in pairs. Look at the picture again. Describe the location of one thing. Say the object your partner is describing.

A: It's on the desk.
B: Is it the lamp?

D Student A – Go to the Communication Hub on page 128.
Student B – Go to the Communication Hub on page 132.

LISTENING

A PREPARE TO LISTEN Read the information about a studio apartment and answer the questions.

1 Where is the studio?
2 What is near the studio?
3 How can you get more information?

NYC RENTALS
Studio for rent in central Manhattan.
Close to a bus stop and a grocery store.
Must see! Call for an appointment.
646-755-8318

Predicting

Before you listen, try to think about which topics will be in the conversation. Predicting helps to make the information easier to understand.

B PREDICT Look at the form in Exercise D. Check (✓) the topics that you think you will hear in the conversation.

☐ location ☐ neighbors ☐ number of rooms ☐ pets ☐ money ☐ stores ☐ size

6.5 **C** LISTEN FOR GIST Listen to the conversation and check your answers to Exercise B. Does the man decide to rent the apartment?

6.5 **D** LISTEN FOR DETAIL Listen to the conversation again. Complete the form with the correct information.

STUDIO FOR RENT

Address: ________ East 23rd Street
Time to bus stop: ________ minutes
Furniture:
☐ desk ☐ chair ☐ bookshelf
☐ lamp ☐ closet ☐ couch
☐ armchair ☐ bed
Window with view of ________
Bathroom: **yes**/**no** Kitchen: **yes**/**no**
Price per month: ________

6.5 **E** LISTEN FOR DETAIL Listen again. Why doesn't the man like the room?

GRAMMAR

is there / are there question forms

A Complete the sentences with the correct form of *be* and the words in the box.

a bathroom (✓) buses (✓) chairs (✗) a kitchen (✗)

1 Is there ___ ___________?
Yes, there ___________.
2 Are there any ___________?
Yes, there ___________.
3 Is there ___ ___________?
No, there ___________.
4 Are there any ___________?
No, there ___________.

B WORK IT OUT Choose the correct options to complete the rules. Use the examples in Exercise A to help you.

is there / are there question forms

To make *yes/no* questions, we put *is* or *are* [1]***before / after*** *there*.

We use *any* in questions with [2]***singular / plural*** nouns.

We [3]***use / don't use*** the contracted form of *there is* (*there's*) in short answers.

C Go to the **Grammar Hub** on **page 108**.

D SPEAK Work in pairs. Ask your partner about their room at home. Use the words in the box.

books bookshelf clock cushions desk lamp pictures window

A: Are there any books in your room?
B: Yes, there are a lot of books. They're on a bookshelf.

PRONUNCIATION

Vowel sounds: /ʌ/ and /e/

6.6 **A** Listen to the sounds /ʌ/ and /e/.

/ʌ/ rug /e/ bed

6.7 **B** Listen and circle the words with the same vowel sound as the word in bold.

1 **/ʌ/ rug**
son run song some love blog
2 **/e/ bed**
get clean red sad bread head

6.8 **C** Listen and circle the word you hear.

1 There's a *bag / bug* on the floor.
2 This is a *bad room / bedroom*.
3 Is there a *pen / pan* in the kitchen?
4 Be careful with that *cut / cat*!

SPEAKING HUB

A PREPARE You want to rent a room from your partner. Student A – Stay on this page. Student B – Go to the **Communication Hub** on **page 130**. Read the description of what you need. Write five questions to ask your partner.

a desk	*Is there a desk?*
chairs	
a lamp	
a TV	
near a bus stop or train station	
near a grocery store	

B DISCUSS Ask your partner questions about their room. Find out if it is the right place for you.

A: Can I ask about the room for rent?
B: Yes, of course. How can I help you?
A: Is it near a bus stop?
B: No, it isn't. But there's a train station ten minutes away.

C REPEAT Answer your partner's questions. Use the information in the advertisement.

Your room:

- Comfortable room in quiet area.
- Near museums, theaters and restaurants.
- Large window with view of the street.
- Bed, table, chair and lamp included.
- Free internet included.

$200 per week

D REPORT Tell the class about the room.

I like / don't like my partner's room because …

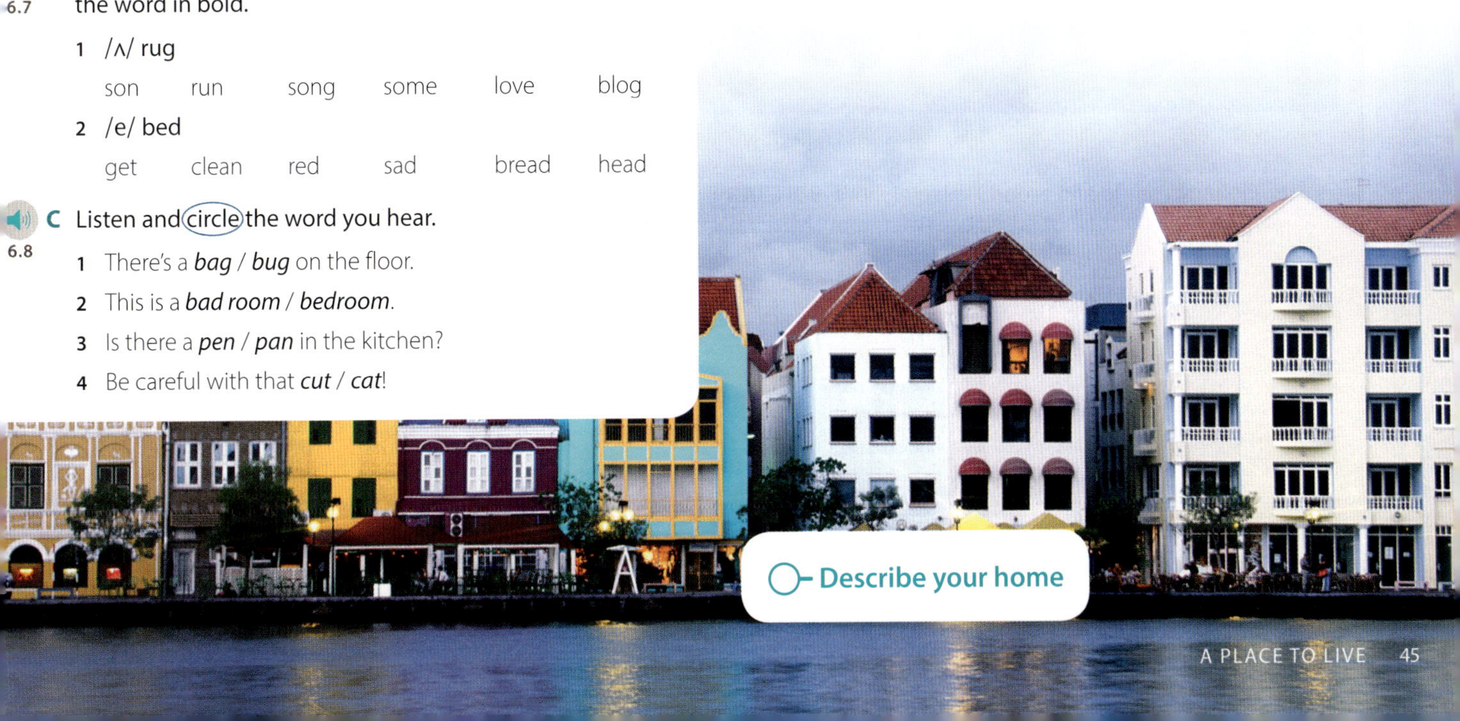

Describe your home

6.3 Left or right?

F – ask for and give directions

COMPREHENSION

A Watch the video. Are the sentences true (T) or false (F)? Correct the false sentences.

1 Gaby wants to take photos in the park. *T / F*
2 Sam gives directions to the park. *T / F*
3 Newton Green park is near Sam's Café. *T / F*
4 The three men in the café are friends. *T / F*
5 Gaby asks her phone for directions. *T / F*

B Watch the video and match the locations of the park (a, b or c) with the three men (1, 2 and 3).

Man 1 ___

Man 2 ___

Man 3 ___

USEFUL PHRASES

A Who says it? Sam, Man 1, Man 2 or Man 3?

1 Yes, it's very near. ________
2 OK everybody, let's just relax. ________
3 You're both wrong. ________
4 Yes, calm down! ________
5 I'm not sure. ________

B Complete the conversation with useful phrases from Exercise A.

Gaby: Is there a park near here?
Sam: A park … [1] ________
Man 1: Actually, there is a park near here. Newton Green.
Gaby: Newton Green.
Man 1: [2] ________ Go out of the café, turn left, then cross the road, then turn right.
Man 2: No, no, no. Go out of the café, turn left and cross the road. But then, turn left, not right.
Man 1: No, it's right.
Man 2: No, it's left.
Man 1: Right.
Man 2: Left.
Sam: [3] ________
Man 3: [4] ________
[5] ________

C 00:24–01:21 Watch part of the video again and check your answers.

GABY

SAM

LUCY

FUNCTIONAL LANGUAGE
Asking for and giving directions

A Complete the phrases with the words in the box.

Cross	Go	left	near	on	out	there	Turn

Asking for directions

Is [1] __________ a park [2] __________ here?

Giving directions

Go [3] __________ of the café.	
Turn [4] __________.	
[5] __________ right.	
[6] __________ the street.	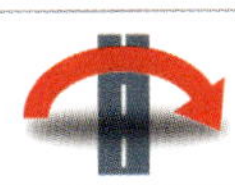
[7] __________ straight ahead.	
The park is [8] __________ your left.	

B Look at the map of the town in the Speaking section. Complete the correct directions to go from Sam's Café to Newton Green.

Go [1] __________ of the café and turn [2] __________. Then turn [3] __________ and go [4] __________. Then turn [5] __________ and then turn [6] __________. The park is on your [7] __________.

PRONUNCIATION

6.9 **A** Listen to the conversation and notice how the underlined words are stressed.

James: Is there a restaurant near here?
Sarah: Yes. Go out of the café and turn right. Then turn right and go straight ahead. Then turn right again and then turn left. The restaurant is on your left.
James: So, I go out of the café and turn right.
Sarah: Yes. Then turn right and go straight ahead.
James: Then turn right again and then left and the restaurant is on my left. Perfect.

6.9 **B** Work in pairs. Listen again and repeat the conversation. Copy the stress.

C **SPEAK** Work in pairs. Practice the conversation in Exercise A.

SPEAKING

A **PREPARE** Work in pairs. Take turns asking for and giving directions from Sam's Café. Use the map below.

A: Is there a movie theater near here?
B: Yes. Go out of Sam's Café and turn left. Then turn left and then left again. The movie theater is on your left.

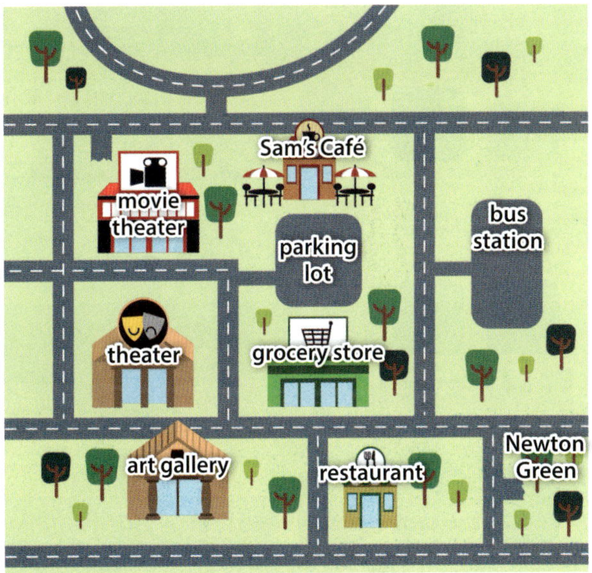

B **PRACTICE** Work in groups of three. Write and practice a conversation. Use the map above or use a local map. Include three or more useful phrases.

Student A
- Ask for directions to a place on the map.

Student B
- Give wrong directions.

Student C
- Disagree and give the correct directions.

C **PRESENT** Perform your conversation for the class. Which conversation is the best?

Ask for and give directions

6 Writing

Write a review of a café

W– using *because*

A Work in pairs. Describe the picture. Use the words in the box to help you.

chair floor lamp table wall window

B Read the text. Why did the writer write it?

a to ask people to visit the café

b to say what he thinks about the café

c to tell the story of his visit to the café

Amazing hot chocolate! ★★★★☆

I love this café because it's modern and clean. There are really cool chairs and tables. The hot chocolate is excellent, but it's a little expensive! It's usually very busy and I sometimes wait 20 minutes or more for my hot chocolate. There's free internet so it's the perfect place to read your emails and text messages.

♡ 7 ⇄ 2

C Read the text again. What are the positive and negative things about the café?

Positive	Negative

Using *because*

We use *because* to give reasons and answer the question *why?*

I love this café ***because*** it's modern and clean.

D SPEAK Work in pairs. What is your opinion of this café?

WRITING

A PREPARE Think of a café that you like or don't like. Complete the table with your reasons.

Like	Dislike

B WRITE Write a short review of your café. Use the review in Exercise B as a model.

C PRESENT Read your review to your partner. Listen to your partner. When they finish ask questions for more information.

Write a review of a café

Unit 6 Review

GRAMMAR

A Choose the correct options to complete the sentences.

1 *There's / There are* three theaters in my town.

2 *Are there / There are* any art galleries?

3 There aren't any *stores / park*.

4 *There's / Is there* a new café near my home.

5 A: Is there a market?
B: Yes, *there is / there's*.

B Complete the conversation with the correct form of *there is* or *there are*.

Aya: Please tell me about your new apartment. 1 ________________ a living room?

Kay: Yes, 2 ________________ a living room. 3 ________________ also two bedrooms.

Aya: 4 ________________ any stores nearby?

Kay: No, 5 ________________. But 6 ________________ a large grocery store near the station.

VOCABULARY

A Complete the words to describe places in a town.

1 I always buy fresh food at the m _ _ _ _ _.

2 My friends sometimes play soccer in the p _ _ _.

3 They usually stay in a h _ _ _ _ when they go on vacation.

4 I go to the s _ _ _ _ _ _ every morning at 8 am to get the train.

5 We sometimes eat dinner at a r _ _ _ _ _ _ _ _ _ near our house.

B Complete the sentences with prepositions of place and words for furniture.

There are two chairs and a desk in this room. There's a cushion 1 ________________ one chair. There's a bag 2 ________________ the other chair. There's a 3 ________________ and a 4 ________________ on the desk. There are books on the 5 ________________. There's a mirror 6 ________________ the wall. There are some clothes in the 7 ________________. There's a small 8 ________________ on the floor.

7 SKILLS

If you think you can do it, you can.
John Burroughs

Performer with the Chinese State Circus, London, England.

OBJECTIVES

- talk about your abilities
- talk about people's talents
- make polite requests
- write a competition entry

Work with a partner. Discuss the questions.

1 Look at the picture. What can you see?

2 Look at the picture again. Choose the correct options to complete the description.

There is a [1]*man* / *woman*. He has a lot of things on his [2]*head* / *hand*. He has [3]*black* / *gray* hair. There's a [4]*bag* / *bird* at the top.

3 Read the quote. Do you agree?

7.1 What can you do?

Talk about your abilities

G *can/can't* **P** *can/can't*: /æ/ and /ə/ **V** abilities

READING

A PREPARE TO READ Work in pairs. Look at the pictures (a–c) in the article and discuss the questions.

1 What can you see in the pictures?
2 What sport do you think each picture shows?

B READ FOR MAIN IDEA Read the article quickly. Choose the correct options.

1 This article is about what some …
  a animals can't do. b people can do.
2 This writer talks to three people about …
  a their abilities. b their pets.
3 The people can do …
  a amazing things. b useful things.

C READ FOR KEY INFORMATION Read the article again. Choose the correct numbers to complete the sentences.

2 4 (x2) 6 80 500

1 Luis can climb __________ meters up a mountain in __________ hours.
2 Seon-Yeong can fly for __________ kilometers. She can be in the air for __________ minutes.
3 Ireen can swim down __________ meters. She can be underwater for __________ minutes.

ANIMALS VS HUMANS

As we all know, animals can do many things that humans can't do. Birds can fly, fish can swim and breathe underwater, and monkeys can climb. Humans can't. Or can we? This week we talk to three amazing humans about their abilities.

Interviewer: Luis, what exactly is a free climber?

A free climber doesn't use ropes to help them climb, only to stop them from falling. Sometimes it's a little bit dangerous. I can't climb for very long because it's difficult and I get tired. I can climb about 500 meters in four hours.

Interviewer: Seon-Yeong, can you really fly?

Yes, I can! I'm a wingsuit flyer in my free time. Birds take off from the ground, but I can't. I jump from somewhere really high, like the top of a mountain or from a plane. I can fly for about four kilometers, and I'm usually in the air for two minutes.

Interviewer: Ireen, you're a free diver – how long can you stay underwater?

I can hold my breath for about six minutes. I don't have an air tank, so I am very careful when I dive. I can dive about 80 meters down and then I need to come up again. I love it, it's so quiet underwater!

a

b

c
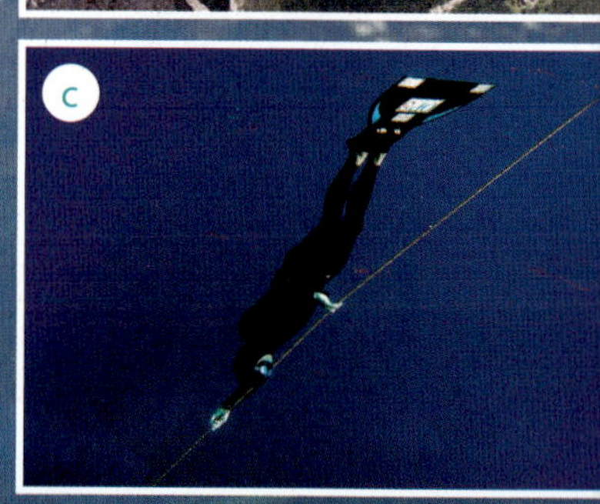

D READ FOR DETAIL Read the article again. Are the statements true (T) or false (F)?

1 Animals and humans have some of the same skills. *T / F*
2 Free climbing is very dangerous. *T / F*
3 Wingsuit flyers need to take off from a high place. *T / F*
4 Free divers don't take any extra air when they go underwater. *T / F*

E SPEAK Work in groups. Answer the questions

1 Which sport in the text do you want to try?
2 Are there other sports you want to try?

I want to try wingsuit flying – it looks really fun!

GRAMMAR

can/can't

A WORK IT OUT Read the examples from the article. Choose the correct option to complete the rule.

Animals can do many things that humans can't do.

A: Can you really fly?

B: Yes, I can!

> ***can/can't***
>
> We use *can/can't* to talk about ***abilities*** / ***routines***.

B WORK IT OUT Read the examples again. Choose the correct options to complete the rules.

> ***can/can't***
>
> 1 After *can* and *can't* we use a **verb with *to*** / **verb without *to***. We always use the same form of the verb with all subjects.
>
> 2 We **use** / **don't use** *do* and *don't* in questions and negative sentences with *can/can't*.

C Go to the **Grammar Hub** on **page 110**.

D PRACTICE Order the words to make questions and answers.

1 A: you / swim / can

______________________________?

B: can / yes, / I

______________________________.

2 A: a monkey / fly / can

______________________________?

B: no, / can't / it

______________________________.

3 A: you / can / what / do

______________________________?

B: can / a mountain / I / climb

______________________________.

4 A: which / can / live / animal / underwater

______________________________?

B: live / can / underwater / a fish

______________________________.

PRONUNCIATION

can/can't: /æ/ and /ə/

7.1 **A** Listen and repeat the sounds, words and examples.

/æ/ can	**A:** Can you climb? **B:** Yes, I can.
/ə/ can	**A:** What can you do? **B:** I can swim.
/æ/ can't	I can't fly.

B SPEAK Work in pairs. Ask questions like the ones in Exercise A. Give answers that are true for you.

A: Can you climb?
B: Yes, I can. I can't climb a mountain. I can climb a tree! What can you do?

VOCABULARY

Abilities

A Complete the sentences with the verbs in the box.

cook dance draw juggle sing ski

1 Helia can ______.

4 Pablo can ______.

2 Gus can ______.

5 Mira can ______.

3 Gina can ______.

6 Alex can ______.

B Match the verbs (1–6) to the nouns (a–f) to make phrases.

1 drive ___	3 do ___	5 ride ___
2 play ___	4 paint ___	6 speak ___
a French	c the guitar	e a car
b yoga	d a picture	f a motorcycle

C Write the correct phrases from Exercise B under each picture.

a

____

b

____

c

____

d

____

e

____

f

____

D Go to the **Vocabulary Hub** on **page 125**.

SPEAKING

A PREPARE You are going to interview your classmates. Work in pairs. Choose five abilities from the ideas below or use your own ideas.

ride a motorcycle draw climb a mountain swim juggle ski play the piano speak Spanish dance cook drive a car

B PLAN Write one question about each ability you chose.

Can you ride a motorcycle?

C PRACTICE Go around the class. Find people who can do each activity on your list.

A: Can you ride a motorcycle?
B: Yes, I can.

D REPORT Work in groups. Tell the group the results of your survey.

A: Three people can ride a motorcycle.
B: Six people can draw.

Talk about your abilities

7.2 He's amazing!

Talk about people's talents

S listening for pronoun reference V adjectives G possessive 's P possessive 's

Sheku Kanneh-Mason

LISTENING

A PREPARE TO LISTEN Look at the picture. Choose the correct words to complete the sentences. There are three words you don't need.

cellos dancers guitars musicians pianos violins

1 These people are ______.
2 Two people have ______.
3 Three people have ______.

7.2 **B LISTEN FOR GIST** Listen to a radio show. Find and correct three mistakes in the summary.

Sheku Kanneh-Mason is a musician. He has eight brothers and sisters. They all study at the Royal Academy of Music. Their parents play musical instruments.

Listening for pronoun reference

We use pronouns (*I, you, we, they, he, she, it, this, that*) and adverbs (*there, here*) so we don't need to repeat names of people and places. Listen for a name or a place and think about the pronoun or adverb the speaker will use in their next sentence.

Sheku Kanneh-Mason*'s an amazing musician.* ***He****'s the winner of the 2016 BBC Young Musician of the Year Award.*

Oliver: Are they students at the ***Royal Academy of Music****, as well?*

Carrie: No, they don't go ***there*** *– not yet anyway.*

7.2 **C LISTEN FOR DETAIL** Listen again. Match the names of people and places (1–6) with their connection to Sheku (a–f).

1 Braimah a his parents
2 Isata b his sister
3 Kadiatu and Stuart c his brother
4 Nottingham d where he lives
5 Royal Academy of Music e where he studies

D SPEAK Work in pairs. Answer the questions.

1 Can you play a musical instrument? Which one(s)?
2 Who is talented in your family? What can they do?

VOCABULARY
Adjectives

A Read the sentences from the radio show.
The underlined word in sentence 1 is an adjective.
Underline the adjectives in sentences 2 and 3.

1 *Every day we talk about an interesting person.*
2 *Today's person is a young musician.*
3 *It's difficult to find the time to play an instrument …*

B Match the adjectives in Exercise A with their definitions.

1 Someone who is ______ has lived for only a short time.
2 Something that is ______ is not easy to do or understand.
3 Something, or someone, that is ______ is exciting and unusual.

C Read the sentences in Exercise A again. Choose the correct option to complete the rules.

1 We use adjectives ***before*** / ***after*** a noun.
2 We use adjectives on their own ***before*** / ***after*** the verb *be*.

D Underline the adjectives in these sentences.

1 He's an amazing musician.
2 My sisters are all great swimmers.
3 Fionn and Carla are both bad dancers.
4 Lois's singing is terrible.
5 Oliver's a talented artist.
6 Juan's dad is awful at cooking.
7 This is a boring book.
8 I eat a lot of healthy food.

E Work in pairs. Complete the table with the adjectives in Exercise D. Are they positive (+) or negative (–)?

Positive	Negative
amazing	

F SPEAK Use the adjectives in the box to complete the sentences so they are true for you. Tell your partner.

amazing bad boring difficult easy good OK talented terrible

1 I'm a(n) ______ musician.
2 I think it's ______ to play the cello.
3 I think it's ______ to have a big family.
4 I think music with violins and cellos is ______.

GRAMMAR
Possessive 's

A Read the sentences from the radio show. Underline the words with the possessive 's.

1 Braimah is Sheku's brother.
2 Sheku's parents' names are Kadiatu and Stuart.

B WORK IT OUT Choose the correct option to complete the rule.

We use 's and ' to say that someone or something *belongs to* / *happens to* someone or something.

C WORK IT OUT Read the sentences again. Add 's or ' to complete the rules and examples.

Possessive 's

We use [1] ____ after singular nouns: *Sheku is Braimah* [2] ____ *brother.*
We use [3] ____ after plural nouns ending in -s: *His sisters* [4] ____ *names are Isata, Konya, Jeneba, Aminatu and Mariatu.*

D PRACTICE Add 's or ' in the correct place to complete the sentences.

1 My mother name is Kali. *My mother's name is Kali.*
2 Luke favorite instrument is the violin.
3 My two cousins house is in the city.
4 Alice's parents names are Olive and Oscar.
5 All of the musicians instruments are in the next room.
6 Alberto is Carlos brother.

E WORK IT OUT Read the information and choose the correct options.

Possessive 's, *is* and *has*

We also use 's as a short form of *is* or *has*.
His name's Sheku Kanneh-Mason. (= his name [1]*is / has*)
He's done his homework. (= he [2]*is / has*)

F PRACTICE Choose the correct meaning of 's in these sentences.

1	Mark's my father.	*is / has / possessive 's*
2	My father's name is Mark.	*is / has / possessive 's*
3	Mark's gone to the store.	*is / has / possessive 's*

G Go to the Grammar Hub on page 110.

H SPEAK Work in pairs. Tell your partner about the following things …

- your family
- your home
- your hobby

My sister is a musician. My home is in Costa Rica. My hobby is swimming.

I SPEAK Work in groups. Tell them about your partner. Use possessive 's.

Erica's sister is a musician. Erica's home is in Costa Rica. Erica's hobby is swimming.

PRONUNCIATION
Possessive 's

A 7.3 Listen to how we say the *s* at the end of each of the names in the table.

/z/	/s/	/ɪz/
Aminata's	Albert's	Angus's
____	____	____

B 7.4 Listen to three more names. Write them in the table.

Alex's Anna's Juliet's

C 7.5 Choose the correct pronunciation for the possessive 's at the end of the names. Listen, check and repeat.

1	Marcus's	/z/	/s/	/ɪz/	4	Carlos's	/z/	/s/	/ɪz/
2	Tom's	/z/	/s/	/ɪz/	5	Bec's	/z/	/s/	/ɪz/
3	Junko's	/z/	/s/	/ɪz/	6	Max's	/z/	/s/	/ɪz/

SPEAKING HUB

A Work in pairs. Student A – Stay on this page. Student B – Go to the Communication Hub on page 133.

B PREPARE Read the information about this person. Write questions to find the missing information.

HIFUMI ABE is from [1] ____________. He is good at judo. He is a world champion. His sister's name is [2] ____________. She is good at judo, too. [3] ____________ is the 2017 Junior World Champion. They are the winners of the 2017 Tokyo Grand Slam.

1 Where is Hifumi from? 2 What …? 3 Who …?

C DISCUSS Work in pairs. Ask your partner questions to complete the missing information. Answer your partner's questions.

D REPEAT Repeat with the information below.

JONATHAN BROWNLEE is from England. He is good at [1] ____________. He can swim, ride a bicycle and run – and he's fast! His brother is good at [2] ____________. His brother's name is Alistair. They both have [3] ____________.

E REFLECT Think of another amazing person. Tell your partner about them.

Talk about people's talents

Café Hub

7.3 New hair

F– make polite requests

COMPREHENSION

A ▶ 00.54–02:41 Watch the first part of the video and answer the questions.

1 Who is Lisa?
2 What sort of hairstyle does Gaby want?
3 What do you think Gaby's new hairstyle is like?

B ▶ 02:42–02:57 Watch the end of the video. What is Gaby's new hairstyle? Do you like it?

C When Gaby says *Wow!* what does she mean?

1 I love it.
2 I hate it.
3 It's OK.

D Complete the sentences with the words in the box.

concert hairstyle Lisa's Hair magazine Spain three o'clock

a Gaby arrives at the hairdresser's at ________________.
b Lucy invites Gaby to a friend's ________________.
c Gaby calls ________________.
d The hairdresser loves ________________.
e Gaby wants to change her ________________.
f Gaby reads a ________________.

E ▶ Put the events (a–f) in Exercise D in the correct order (1–6). Then watch the video again and check your answers.

FUNCTIONAL LANGUAGE

Making polite requests

A Underline the polite phrases. Who said it?

1 So, Gaby what ***do you want*** / ***would you like***?
 a Gaby b Lisa
2 ***I'd like*** / ***I want*** something different, please.
 a Gaby b Lisa

B Complete the phrases by putting the word in parentheses in the correct place.

1 Three o'clock is fine. Can I *have* your phone number, please? (have)
2 I'd like book an appointment, please. (to)
3 Is Lisa's Hair? (that)
4 you have time today? (Do)
5 Yes, is. (it)
6 Yes, today's good. What time would you to come? (like)
7 Yeah sure! When you like to come? (would)

GABY

SAM

LUCY

C Complete the conversation with the phrases from Exercise B.

1 *Is that Lisa's Hair?*

Yes, 2 ______________.

3 ______________

4 ______________

5 ______________

6 ______________

7 *Three o'clock?*

8 ______________

Sure.

D ▶ 01:01–02:05 Watch part of the video again and check your answers to Exercises B and C.

PRONUNCIATION

7.6 **A** Listen to the conversation and notice how the intonation goes up (↗) or goes down (↘) in questions.

Ben:	Is this Dr. Jones? (↗)
Dr. Jones:	Yes, it is.
Ben:	Can I book an appointment, please? (↗)
Dr. Jones:	Sure. When would you like to come? (↘)
Ben:	Do you have time today? (↗)
Dr. Jones:	Yes, today's good. What time? (↘)
Ben:	Is two o'clock OK? (↗)
Dr. Jones:	Two o'clock's fine. Can I have your phone number, please? (↗)

7.6 **B** Listen again and repeat the conversation. Copy the intonation.

SPEAKING

A PREPARE Work in pairs. Replace the red words in Pronunciation Exercise A with different people, times and places. Use the ideas below or your own ideas. Practice the dialogue.

Person	Day	Time
Dr. Smith	tomorrow	noon
Johanna Mendelsohn, mechanic	Monday	two thirty
Mr. Roberts, bank manager	next Tuesday	four o'clock

B PLAN Make appointments with other students in the class. Put a check mark (✓) next to the six times when you are free today and tomorrow.

	TODAY	TOMORROW
09:00		
10:00		
11:00		
12:00		
1:00		
2:00		
3:00		
4:00		
5:00		
6:00		
7:00		
8:00		

C PRACTICE Go around the class and make appointments with other students. Then change roles and do the activity again.

A: Is this (name of person)?
B: Yes, it is.
A: Can I book an appointment, please?
B: Yes. When would you like to come?
A: Is today at 11 o'clock OK?
B: Sorry, I'm not free. Is 12 o'clock OK?
A: 12 o'clock's fine.

Make polite requests

7 Writing

Write a competition entry

W– using commas in lists

A Read the two texts. Then choose the correct option to complete the sentence.

The texts are applications for a *talent competition* / *sports competition*.

B Work in pairs. Complete the applications with the words in the box.

artist cello dance person picture Spanish

Anyone Can Do It!

Name: Imelda Suarez **Age:** 29

About you: I'm Imelda and I'm from Spain. I love music and I can play the guitar, the piano and the [1] ________. I can also sing and [2] ________. I also love languages and I can speak [3] ________, Italian and English.

Anyone Can Do It!

Name: Lucas Johnson **Age:** 32

About you: I'm Canadian, but I live in Mexico. I really love art. I'm a(n) [4] ________, and I'm really fast! I can draw, and I can paint a(n) [5] ________ of any animal, [6] ________ or thing, and I can do it in one or two minutes!

Using commas in lists

We use a comma (,) when we write more than two words in a list. We don't usually use a comma before *and*.

I can play the guitar, the piano and the cello.

C Add the missing commas to these sentences.

1. My brother can speak English Turkish and Arabic.
2. Kyle swims runs and rides his bike every week.
3. I go to Spanish classes on Mondays Wednesdays and Fridays.

WRITING

WRITE Imagine that this is your application for the talent show. Complete the missing information. Write a short paragraph. Use commas.

Anyone Can Do It!

Name: ________

Age: ________

What can you do?

I can … ________

Write a competition entry

Unit 7 Review

GRAMMAR

A Choose the correct options to complete the sentences.

1. My brother *can* / *can to* swim underwater for three minutes.
2. Lyra can *jump* / *jumps* six meters.
3. **A:** *Do you can* / *Can you* draw?
   B: Yes, I *can* / *draw*.
4. What *do you can* / *can you do*?
5. I *can't drive* / *drive can't* a car, but I *do* / *can* ride a motorcycle.

B Find and correct the mistake in each sentence.

1. Johns brother can play the piano.
2. My sisters names are Jo and Leah.
3. Alexs' hobby is wingsuit flying.
4. What are your parent's names?
5. My friends' an amazing dancer.
6. Paulo's friends' played the cello.

VOCABULARY

A Complete the phrases with the correct letters.

1. p _a_ i _n_ t a p _i_ c t _u_ _r_ _e_
2. p ___ y the g ___ t ___ r
3. d r ___ v ___ a c ___
4. s p ___ k T ___ r k ___ s h
5. r ___ d ___ a b ___ c ___ c ___ e
6. ___ l ___ y s ___ c ___ r

B Complete the sentences with the adjectives in the box.

boring difficult good long old terrible

1. Niall's a ________ musician. He can play a lot of instruments.
2. Yoga is ________. I can't do it.
3. My grandmother is ________. She's 97.
4. My Spanish is ________. I can't say anything.
5. I do yoga for a ________ time every day. I sometimes do it for four hours.
6. I don't like shopping at the grocery store. I think it's ________.

8 THE HERE AND NOW

Be happy for this moment.
This moment is your life.
Omar Khayyam

A man in front of the Northern Lights, Alaska.

OBJECTIVES

- describe what people are doing
- talk about clothes
- shop for clothes
- write a short message

Work with a partner. Discuss the questions.

1 Look at the picture. Which words from the box describe it?

amazing	boring	beautiful	blue	cold
day	green	warm	night	ugly

2 Would you like to visit this place? Why/ Why not?

3 Read the quote. Tell your partner three good things about today.

8.1 What's he doing?

Describe what people are doing

G present progressive **V** verb phrases **P** different ways to pronounce *a*

LISTENING

A PREPARE TO LISTEN Look at the pictures. Match the things (1–6) with the correct picture (a–d).

1 a bench *b*
2 a book ____
3 coffee ____
4 a phone ____
5 a sandwich ____
6 trees ____

B PREPARE TO LISTEN Look at the comic strip again. Choose the correct options.

1 Picture a: The man is talking to a *woman* / *police officer*.
2 Picture b: The man is having lunch *with friends* / *alone*.
3 Picture c: The man is lying *under a tree* / *on a bench*.
4 Picture d: The man is looking at his *watch* / *phone*.

8.1 **C LISTEN FOR THE MAIN IDEA** Listen to a conversation. Put the pictures (a–d) in the correct order.

D SPEAK Work in pairs. Discuss the questions.

1 Do the police have the right man?
2 What item of clothing is the right man wearing?

GRAMMAR

Present progressive

8.2 **A** Listen to a part of the conversation again. Complete the missing words.

Officer A: Can you see the [1] ____________?
Officer B: Yes. I'm watching him [2] ____________.
Officer A: What's he doing?
Officer B: He's having [3] ____________.
Officer A: Is he talking to [4] ____________?
Officer B: No, he isn't. He's by himself.
Officer A: Is he in a [5] ____________?
Officer B: No, he's sitting on a [6] ____________. He's eating a [7] ____________ and drinking [8] ____________.

B WORK IT OUT Read the conversation in Exercise A. Underline the verbs that end with *-ing*. Choose the correct option to complete the rule.

We use present progressive (verb + *-ing*) to talk about *right now* / *every day*.

C WORK IT OUT Read the examples of the present progressive in the conversation again. Choose the correct options.

Present progressive

1 We make present progressive with *subject* + *be* + *to* + *verb* / *subject* + *be* + *verb* + *-ing*.
2 In questions, the subject (*I, you, he, she, it …*) goes *before* / *after* be.
3 In short answers, we use *subject* + *be* / *subject* + *be* + *verb* + *-ing*.

D WORK IT OUT Complete the table with the correct form of the verbs in the box. Use Exercise A to help you.

eat have sit

Verb (base form)	Spelling rule	Verb + *-ing*
do watch [1] ____	Verb + *-ing*	doing watching [4] ____
live [2] ____	Verb (without *-e*), + *-ing*	living [5] ____
get [3] ____	Verb (add extra last consonant) + *-ing*	getting [6] ____

E Go to the **Grammar Hub** on **page 112**.

F SPEAK Work in pairs. Choose a picture from the comic strip but don't tell your partner which one. Describe it to your partner. Which picture is it?

A: I can see a man.
B: What's he doing?
A: He's sitting on a bench. He's …
B: Is it picture …?

VOCABULARY
Verb phrases

A Choose the correct verbs to complete the phrases. Use each verb only once.

go have look meet read take talk watch

1 ________ a friend

2 ________ at your phone

3 ________ a selfie

4 ________ a good time

5 ________ the newspaper

6 ________ a movie

7 ________ to the bank

8 ________ to a friend

B Match the verbs from Exercise A with the words and phrases.

1 *have* lunch / a meeting / coffee
2 ________ TV / a soccer game / someone do something
3 ________ a book / a message / a magazine
4 ________ out / to the library / shopping
5 ________ to a teacher / on the phone / about something
6 ________ a photo / a break / a taxi
7 ________ at a picture / in the mirror / at someone
8 ________ someone at a party / at nine o'clock / at the station

PRONUNCIATION
Different ways to pronounce *a*

8.3 **A** Listen and repeat the words in the table.

/æ/	/eɪ/	/ɔː/	/ɑ/
have	take	walk	watch

8.4 **B** Listen to the words in the box and put them in the correct place in the table.

call catch fall match play stay want wash

8.5 **C** Listen and complete the questions.

1 What do you ________: ball games or board games?
2 Who do you ________ to every day?
3 What do you usually ________ for lunch?
4 What do you ________ to ________: a soccer game or a movie?

D **SPEAK** Work with a partner. Ask the questions in Exercise C. Give full answers.

SPEAKING

Work in pairs. Student A – Look at the instructions below. Student B – Go to the **Communication Hub** on **page 131**.

Student A

- Look at the picture.
- Describe the people and what they are doing to your partner.
- Listen to your partner's description of their picture.
- Find six differences.

Describe what people are doing

8.2 The gray coat

Talk about clothes

V clothes **P** vowel sounds: /iː/, /ɜː/, /uː/ and /ɔː/ **S** identifying key words **G** adjective order

VOCABULARY
Clothes

A Look at Person 1 in the picture. What clothes is he wearing? Choose words from the box to complete the description.

shorts sneakers socks T-shirt

He's wearing a white [1] ________ and blue [2] ________. He's wearing red [3] ________ and white [4] ________. He also has a green backpack.

B Go to the **Vocabulary Hub** on **page 125**.

C **SPEAK** Work in pairs. Choose someone in the picture. Ask and answer questions. Who is your partner describing?

A: She's wearing a dress.
B: Is she wearing a hat?
A: Yes, she is.

PRONUNCIATION
Vowel sounds: /iː/, /ɜː/, /uː/ and /ɔː/

8.6 **A** Complete the sentences with a word in the box that has the same sound as the underlined letters. Listen and check.

a coat ~~a hat~~ jeans a shirt shorts a suit

1 Hannah's wearing a cap. Izzie's wearing *a hat*.
2 Ally's wearing a skirt and ________.
3 Paulo's wearing ________ and shoes.

8.7 **B** Listen to the words for clothes. Then listen and repeat.

jeans shirt shoes shorts

8.8 **C** Match the words in the box with the correct vowel sound in questions 1–4. Then listen and check.

bird clean do door green sports who word

1 /iː/ jeans ________ ________
2 /ɜː/ shirt ________ ________
3 /uː/shoes ________ ________
4 /ɔː/ shorts ________ ________

D **SPEAK** Work in pairs. Look around you. Describe different people.

A: Eva's wearing jeans. *B: Elliot's wearing a shirt.*

READING

A **PREPARE TO READ** Look at the picture at the top of the page again. What are the people doing?

B **READ FOR KEY WORDS** Read the messages and look at the picture. Which person (1–11) is Claus? Which person is Imogen?

Claus ___ Imogen ___

Identifying key words

Looking for key words can help you understand the topic of a text or sentence quickly.

*I'm wearing a gray **sweatshirt**. [Topic = clothes]*

Claus

Hi Claus, I'm at the station. Where are you?

I'm here, too. I have the bag, but I can't see you. What are you wearing?

An old blue sweatshirt and a yellow cap.

Sorry, I can't see you. Where are you?

I'm standing near the store. What are you wearing?

A long gray coat.

I think I can see you. Are you wearing a red cap?

Yes, I am.

I can see you! I think the police are watching.

The police? Why are the police watching?

Something's happening at the bank. It's on the radio. The police are looking for a man with a gray coat and a bag with a lot of money.

I have a bag, but it doesn't have any money in it! It's your bag … from the restaurant last night.

I know, thank you! I'm coming over to you now.

C READ FOR SPECIFIC INFORMATION Read the messages again. Answer the questions.

1 Can Imogen see Claus when she arrives at the station?
2 Can Claus see Imogen?
3 Where is Imogen?
4 Why are the police watching Claus?
5 Is Claus the man the police are looking for?
6 Is the bag Claus's bag or Imogen's bag?

D READ FOR DETAIL Read the messages again. Find and correct the five mistakes in the summary.

Claus is at the park. He's meeting Imogen. Claus has a blue coat and a bag. The police are looking for a man with a gray sweatshirt and a bag. Claus has Imogen's coat. There is a lot of money in the bag.

GRAMMAR
Adjective order

A Read the messages in Reading Exercise B again. Underline the adjectives of size or age. Circle the adjectives of color.

B WORK IT OUT Read these sentences from the messages. Choose the correct option to complete the rules.

Adjective order

I'm wearing an old blue sweatshirt and a yellow cap.
I'm wearing a long gray coat.

1 We *can* / *can't* put more than one adjective before a noun.
2 The color adjective usually goes *before* / *after* the adjective for size or age.

C Go to the **Grammar Hub** on **page 112**.

D PRACTICE Rewrite the sentences and add the extra adjectives in parentheses.

1 It's a blue shirt. (new)
It's a new blue shirt.
2 She's wearing an old dress. (green)
______
3 I have a new hat. (red)
______
4 That's a blue skirt. (long)
______

E SPEAK Work in pairs. Describe the clothes in the pictures.

a

b

c

d

big long short small

She's wearing a long yellow coat.

SPEAKING HUB

A PREPARE Imagine you are in these situations. What are you wearing? What are you doing? Write notes.

a You're in the park in the summer.

b You're traveling for business.

c You're at a concert.

B PRACTICE Work in pairs. Choose one of the situations in Exercise A. Your partner is trying to find you, but they can't. Have a phone conversation and describe what you are wearing and what you are doing.

A: What are you wearing?
B: I'm wearing a long red skirt, a white hat and sunglasses.

C REPEAT Find a new partner. Choose a new situation and describe what you're wearing and what you're doing.

Talk about clothes

Café Hub

8.3 Too loud

F– shop for clothes

COMPREHENSION

A ▶ Watch the video and answer the questions.

1 Where are Gaby and Lucy?
2 Who buys something? Why?

B Are the sentences true (T) or false (F)? Correct the false sentences.

1 Gaby is waiting for Lucy. *T / F*
2 Lucy says Gaby's hair is bad. *T / F*
3 The cap seller likes the music. *T / F*
4 Gaby wants to buy a cap. *T / F*
5 There's a blue cap. *T / F*
6 The caps are one size. *T / F*
7 Caps cost £10. *T / F*
8 Gaby needs a small cap. *T / F*

C ▶ Watch the video again and check your answers to Exercise B.

D What do you think of the music? Choose an adjective from the box or use your own ideas.

amazing bad good horrible OK

USEFUL PHRASES

A Match the phrases (1–4) with the pictures (a–d).

1 It's not bad. It's just different. ____
2 Oh, look over there. ____
3 She's joking! ____
4 I have a surprise for you. ____

B Which useful phrase means *She's not serious*?

C ▶ Watch the video again and check your answers to Exercises A and B.

a

b

c

d

GABY

SAM

LUCY

FUNCTIONAL LANGUAGE

Shopping for clothes

A Read the conversation and underline the correct options.

Sales person	Lucy
Can I [1]*see / help*?	We're [2]*just / only* looking, thanks.
No problem.	Actually, I'm [3]*looking / waiting* for a cap.
Sure. We have caps. Lots of them!	Great! Do you have a blue [4]*type / one*?
Yes, we have blue. What [5]*size / color* would you like: small, medium or [6]*big / large*?	Can I [7]*want / have* a medium, please?
Of course.	Perfect. How [8]*much / money* is it?
Ten pounds.	

B 00:45–01:59 Watch part of the video and check your answers.

PRONUNCIATION

8.9 **A** Listen to the conversation and notice how the underlined words are stressed.

Sales person: Can I <u>help</u> you?
Customer: I'm just <u>look</u>ing, <u>thanks</u>.
Sales person: OK, no <u>prob</u>lem.
Customer: Actually, I'm <u>look</u>ing for a <u>T</u>-shirt. Do you have a <u>red</u> one?
Sales person: <u>Yes</u>. What <u>size</u> would you <u>like</u>? <u>Small</u>, <u>me</u>dium or <u>large</u>?
Customer: Can I have a <u>large</u>, please?
Sales person: Of <u>course</u>.
Customer: How <u>much</u> is it?
Sales person: Seven<u>teen</u> <u>dol</u>lars.

8.9 **B** Listen again and repeat the conversation. Copy the stress.

C SPEAK Work in pairs. Practice the conversation.

SPEAKING

A PLAN You are a sales person. Look at the clothes and decide how much each item costs.

$ ______

$ ______

$ ______

$ ______

$ ______

$ ______

B PREPARE You are shopping for clothes. Decide what you want to buy, the color and the size you need.

C PRACTICE Work in pairs. Decide who is the sales person and who is the customer. Have a conversation and buy the clothes you want. Use the conversation in Pronunciation Exercise A to help you.

D REPEAT Change roles and have a new conversation.

Shop for clothes

8 Writing

Write a short message

W using *also* and *too*

A Read the text message conversation between two friends. Choose the correct image for where Mia is.

Hi Mia. What are you doing?

Hi Petra. I'm at a barbecue at Amy's house. It's so nice and sunny today!

Oh great! Who are you with?

I'm with Greg. Lilly's here, too. They're making the food.

What are you doing?!

I'm sitting in the sun and talking to Amy. Do you want to come over?

I can't. I'm shopping with my sister right now. Also, I have to work later. Maybe next time 😉.

a 

b 

B Read the messages again. Answer the questions.

1 Where's Mia?
2 Who's with Mia?
3 What are Greg and Lilly doing?
4 What's Mia doing?
5 Why can't Petra go?

Using *also* and *too*

We use *also* and *too* to say that something is true about more than one person or thing. We usually put *also* at the beginning of a sentence or before the verb. We always put *too* at the end of a sentence.

Also, I have to work later.

Lilly's here, too.

WRITING

WRITE Write a text message conversation between two friends. Choose a situation from the pictures in Exercise A or use your own ideas.

Write a short message

Unit 8 Review

GRAMMAR

A Complete the conversation using short answers and the verbs in parentheses in the present progressive.

A: What [1] ___are___ you ___doing___ (*do*)?
B: I [2] ________ ________ (*eat*) lunch.
A: [3] ________ Michael ________ (*have*) lunch with you?
B: No, he [4] ________. He [5] ________ ________ (*work*) in the library.
A: Who [6] ________ he ________ (*work*) with?
B: He [7] ________ ________ (*not work*) with anyone.

B Order the words to make sentences.

1 is / this / blue / new / my / sweatshirt
This is my new blue sweatshirt.
2 has / an / gray / hat / he / old
________.
3 wearing / a / long / dress / white / she's
________.
4 a / short / coat / brown / the man / wearing / is
________.

VOCABULARY

A Join the halves to make sentences.

1 I'm going — c
2 We're watching
3 Aki and Darren are meeting
4 Luke's reading
5 My sister is having
6 Geri is talking
7 Yannick is looking
8 Luke's taking

a to her friend on the phone.
b a photo with his new camera.
c to a café.
d at the bus station.
e TV at home.
f at clothes in a store.
g lunch.
h a magazine.

B Complete the words for clothes.

1 d _ e _ _
2 sw _ _ _ s _ _ _ _
3 h _ _
4 j _ a _ s
5 s _ _ e _
6 sn _ a _ e _ _

9 LOOKING BACK

Study the past if you would define the future.
Confucius

A statue at Mount Nemrut, Turkey.

OBJECTIVES

- talk about famous people from the past
- talk about people's achievements
- make recommendations
- write a short biography

Work with a partner. Discuss the questions.

1 Look at the picture. Do you want to visit this place?
2 Who is your favorite person from history? Why do you like them?
3 Where can you see statues of famous people in your country?

9.1 Famous faces

Talk about famous people from the past

G simple past: *was/were* **V** dates and years **P** *was he / was she*

LISTENING

A PREPARE TO LISTEN Look at the pictures in *A visit to Madame Tussauds*. Do you know these famous people? Why are they famous?

9.1 **B LISTEN FOR SPECIFIC INFORMATION** Listen and write the missing years (a–d) in *A visit to Madame Tussauds*.

9.1 **C LISTEN FOR SPECIFIC INFORMATION** Listen again and complete the information below.

1 AUDREY HEPBURN

Country: 1 ____________

Jobs: 2 ____________

3 ____________

4 ____________

She was famous for her 5 ____________ clothes.

2 WILLIAM SHAKESPEARE

Country: 6 ____________

Jobs: 7 ____________

8 ____________

9 ____________ of words in everyday English come from his work.

3 MARIE TUSSAUD

Country: 10 ____________

Job: Famous for 11 ____________ in London. 12 ____________

4 NELSON MANDELA

Country: 13 ____________

Job: President for 14 ____________ years.

A VISIT TO MADAME TUSSAUDS

In cities all over the world – in London, Paris, New York and New Delhi – people come to Madame Tussauds to see waxwork statues of famous people from the past and present. Why were they famous? Were they actors? Writers? Or inspirational leaders? Enjoy a visit to Madame Tussauds to find out more about these famous faces.

GRAMMAR
Simple past: *was/were*

A Read the examples from *A visit to Madame Tussauds*. Underline examples of *was* and *were*.

1 Why were they famous?
2 Were they actors?
3 Was she a model?
4 Her movies were very popular.
5 Why was he famous?
6 He was a famous writer.
7 He wasn't just a writer.
8 Photographs weren't common.

B **WORK IT OUT** Complete the table with the sentences from Exercise A.

was/were	Singular	Plural
positive	______	______
negative	______	______
yes/no questions	______	______
wh- questions	______	______

C **WORK IT OUT** Look at Exercises A and B. Complete the rules with *was*, *wasn't*, *were* or *weren't*.

Simple past: *was/were*

1 ______ is the past form of *is*. ______ is the past form of *are*.
2 ______ is the past form of *isn't*. ______ is the past form of *aren't*.
3 We make *yes/no* questions with ______ or ______ + subject.
4 We make *wh-* questions with a question word + ______ or ______.

D Go to the **Grammar Hub** on **page 114**.

E **SPEAK** Work in pairs. Who was your favorite celebrity when you were young? Why were they famous?

VOCABULARY
Dates and years

9.2 **A** Match the numbers (1–6) with the words in the box. Listen and check.

fifth first fourth second sixth third

1 1st ______
2 2nd ______
3 3rd ______
4 4th ______
5 5th ______
6 6th ______

9.3 **B** Listen and write the numbers that you hear.

a ___ b ___ c ___ d ___ e ___
f ___ g ___ h ___ i ___ j ___

9.4 **C** Listen and circle the years you hear.

a 1948 / 1958
b 1909 / 1999
c 2014 / 2040
d 1564 / 1546
e 2002 / 2012
f 1800 / 1900

D **SPEAK** Stand up and walk around. Say the day and month of your birthday to each other. Then stand in order according to your birthday.

PRONUNCIATION
was he / was she

9.5 **A** Read and listen. Draw a line (‿) to show the linked words.

1 Was he a writer?
2 Was she a writer?
3 Where was he born?
4 Where was she born?

9.6 **B** Listen to each question and choose the words you hear.

1 *Was he* / *Was she* an artist?
2 *Was he* / *Was she* an actor?
3 Why *was he* / *was she* famous?
4 When *was he* / *was she* born?

SPEAKING

A **PREPARE** Think of a famous person from the past. Complete the information about him or her.

Man or woman? ______

Country? ______

Job? ______

When were they famous? ______

Why were they famous? ______

B **DISCUSS** Work in pairs. Describe your famous person. Don't say the name of the person. Ask your partner questions. Who is it?

A: He was a singer in The Beatles.
B: John Lennon?

C **REPORT** Tell the class about your famous person.

Talk about famous people from the past

9.2 Voices from the past

Talk about people's achievements

V everyday verbs   S scanning   G simple past: regular verbs   P past tense endings: /d/, /t/ and /ɪd/

VOCABULARY

Everyday verbs

A Look at the pictures. Match the phrases in the box with the correct pictures.

collect stamps   design a building   help a friend
paint a picture   receive a present   start to run
study in college   travel to the city

1 ____________

2 ____________

3 ____________

4 ____________

5 ____________

6 ____________

7 ____________

8 ____________

B **SPEAK** Work in pairs. Use the verbs to make sentences that are true for you.

A: I collect CDs.

B: I travel to Rome every fall for work.

READING

A **PREPARE TO READ** Which heroes from children's stories can you name?

B **READ FOR GIST** Read *Goodnight stories for rebel girls*. Choose the correct options to complete the summary.

Goodnight stories for rebel girls is about ***real women*** / ***women in children's stories***.

Scanning

When you scan a text, you read it to look for specific information. Scanning helps you find information more quickly. Look for key words, names, dates and percentages.

GOODNIGHT STORIES for REBEL GIRLS

What were your favorite stories when you were young? Who were your heroes? How many were girls?

In 2011, the University of Florida studied the number of male and female characters in children's storybooks. There were male characters in every book. But 25 percent had no female characters. And in 37 percent of the books, the female characters didn't talk.

Two Italian women, Elena Favilli and Francesca Cavallo, decided to change this. They wanted to make a book of stories about real women. They asked people for money online to make the book. They received over a million dollars! Here are some of the women in their book:

Maria Sibylla Merian (1647–1717)
Merian was a scientist. She was born in Frankfurt in Germany. When she was a child, she collected butterflies and insects. She discovered many new things about them. She traveled to South America and painted beautiful pictures of nature.

Ada Lovelace (1815–1852)
Lovelace was an English mathematician. She didn't study at public school or college. She studied at home with a teacher. When she was 12, she designed a flying machine. Also, she was the first computer programmer in the world.

Wangari Maathai (1940–2011)
Maathai was a Kenyan politician. She studied at universities in the US and in Germany. She wanted to help people in Kenya, so she and a group of women started to plant trees. They planted hundreds of trees and the trees helped people and nature. She received the Nobel Peace Prize in 2004.

C READ FOR DETAIL Are these statements true (T) or false (F)?

1 There are female characters in all children's books. T / F
2 Some female characters in children's books don't say anything. T / F
3 The writers of *Goodnight stories for rebel girls* are men. T / F
4 Maria Sibylla Merian was a mathematician. T / F
5 Ada Lovelace was a computer programmer. T / F
6 Wangari Maathai was the winner of an important prize. T / F

D SPEAK Work in groups. Discuss the questions.

1 Do you think that this book was a good idea? Why/Why not?
2 Do you think that this book is good for boys, too? Why/Why not?
3 Do girls and boys read the same or different books? Why/Why not?

GRAMMAR

Simple past: regular verbs

A Read the introduction to the article again. Write the simple past: form of the verbs.

1 study ______ 4 ask ______
2 decide ______ 5 receive ______
3 want ______

B Read the section about Ada Lovelace again and <u>underline</u> the negative verb.

C WORK IT OUT Match the two parts of each rule (1–4) with (a–d). Use the examples in Exercises A and B to help you.

Simple past: regular verbs

1 We add *-ed*	a we use *did + not (didn't)* before the verb.
2 We add *-d*	b to verbs ending in *-e*.
3 With verbs ending in *-y*,	c we cut the *-y* and add *-ied*.
4 To form the negative,	d to most verbs.

D Go to the **Grammar Hub** on **page 114**.

PRONUNCIATION

Past tense endings: /d/, /t/ and /ɪd/

9.7 **A** Read and listen to the verbs. Notice how we say the endings.

/d/	/t/	/ɪd/
studied	helped	wanted

9.8 **B** Listen to the verbs and add them to the table in Exercise A.

1 decided
2 asked
3 designed
4 lived
5 started
6 talked
7 collected
8 traveled

SPEAKING HUB

Work in groups. Group A – Stay on this page. Group B – Go to the **Communication Hub** on **page 130**.

A PREPARE Complete the sentences with the past tense of verbs from the box. Then choose the correct information (a, b or c) to complete the sentences.

discover live receive start

1 Larry Page and Segey Brin ______ the company Google in …
a 1998. b 2001. c 2008.
2 John Couch Adams ______ the planet Neptune in …
a 1696. b 1846. c 1906.
3 William Shakespeare ______ in England in the … century.
a 15th b 16th c 17th
4 Malala Yousafzai ______ the Nobel Peace Prize in …
a 2001. b 2014. c 2016.

B PRACTICE Read your sentences to Group B. They will check your answers.

C PRACTICE Listen to Group B's sentences. Check their answers.

Correct sentences:

1 Ibn Battuta **traveled** from Morocco to China in the **14th century**.
2 Gabriel García Márquez **received** the Nobel Prize in Literature in **1982**.
3 Neil Armstrong **walked** on the moon in **1969**.
4 Steve Jobs and Steve Wozniak **designed** the first personal computers in **1976**.

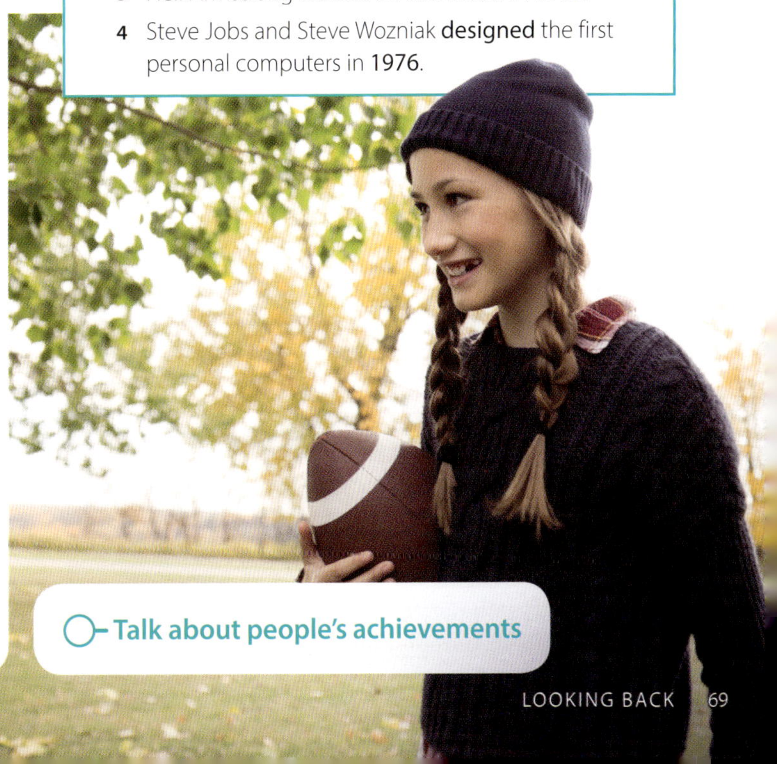

Talk about people's achievements

Café Hub

9.3 Pizza Roma

F– make recommendations

COMPREHENSION

A 00.10–01:14 Watch the first part of the video and choose the correct options to complete the sentences.

1. Sam is *opening* / *closing* the café.
2. Sam *knows* / *doesn't know* Metal Train.
3. Gaby *loves* / *hates* pizza.
4. Pizza Roma is *terrible* / *amazing*.
5. Pizza Roma has *big* / *small* pizzas.
6. The pizzas are *expensive* / *cheap*.
7. Pizza Roma is *near* / *far from* Sam's Café.

B 01:15–01:34 Watch part of the video and choose the correct set of directions from Sam's Café to Pizza Roma.

1  ☐

2 

☐

3  ☐

C 01:35–03:00 Watch the second part of the video. Discuss the questions.

1. What was Gaby's pizza like?
2. Did she eat it?
3. Where did she buy it?
4. What does Gaby eat?
5. What does Lucy do?
6. Where was Lucy's pizza from?

USEFUL PHRASES

A Who says it? Gaby (G) or Sam (S)?

1. I'm afraid I'm closing now. ________
2. Hey! That's a nice cap! ________
3. Ah, I see. ________
4. It's not far. ________
5. It's next to the station. ________
6. I've got it, thanks! ________

Glossary

shop (n) (British) = store (n) (American)

B Match the useful phrases in Exercise A with the meanings.

I understand. [1] ________ [2] ________

I'm sorry … [3] ________

It's near here. [4] ________

I like your … [5] ________

C Replace the underlined phrases with useful phrases from Exercise A.

Gaby: Hi, Sam. [1]I like your T-shirt.

Sam: Thanks. It's from my friend's shop.

Gaby: Where's her shop?

Sam: Oh, [2]it's near here. Just go out the café, turn left, turn left again and it's on your right.

Gaby: Left, left, right. [3]I understand, thanks!

Sam: [4]I'm sorry. I'm going to my yoga class now. It starts in five minutes.

Gaby: Ah, [5]I understand! Bye!

FUNCTIONAL LANGUAGE

Making recommendations

A Complete the phrases with the words in the box. Then watch the video again and check your answers.

Don't | Do you know | There's | You should

Asking for a recommendation

[1] ________ / Is there a good restaurant near here?

Giving a recommendation

[2] ________ / I know a really good pizza restaurant. It's called Pizza Roma.

I was there last week. And the pizza was amazing. It was really big and really cheap.

[3] ________ / Why don't you try it.

[4] ________ / I wouldn't go to Pizza Nova! I went there last week. The pizza was bad! It was really small and really expensive.

B Circle the correct options to complete the conversation.

Liz: [1]*Do you know* / *There's* a good café near here?

Mark: Do you like big breakfasts?

Liz: I love big breakfasts.

Mark: OK, [2]*why don't you* / *there's* a really good café. It's called Tom's Café. I was there this morning. The breakfast is [3]*amazing* / *horrible*. It's really big and really cheap. [4]You *should* / *shouldn't* go there.

Liz: Thanks! Don't go to Rachel's Café. I went there yesterday. The coffee was [5]*amazing* / *terrible*. It was really small and really bad.

Mark: Oh, I see. Thanks.

GABY

SAM

LUCY

PRONUNCIATION

9.9 **A** Listen to the conversation and notice how the underlined words are stressed.

Frank: Do you know a good restaurant near here?
Emily: Do you like sushi?
Frank: I love Japanese food.
Emily: There's a really good Japanese restaurant. It's called Sushirama.
Frank: Great.
Emily: I was there last week. And the sushi was amazing. It was really fresh. You should try it. Don't go to Suzy's Sushi! It's really bad.

9.9 **B** Listen again and repeat the conversation. Copy the stress.

SPEAKING

A PLAN Work in pairs. Read *Restaurants near you*. Discuss the questions.

1. Which restaurant(s) would you like to go to? Why?
2. Which restaurant(s) would you **not** like to go to? Why?

B PREPARE Rewrite the conversation in Pronunciation Exercise A.

- Replace the blue phrases with new ideas from the Functional language section.
- Replace the words in red using the ideas in the reviews below.
- Create some directions and include three or more useful phrases.

C PRACTICE Work in pairs. Practice and then perform your conversation in front of the class.

D REPEAT Choose different restaurants. Change roles and have a new conversation.

Restaurants near you

Moo Burger Bar
★★★★☆
Great fries!

Bob's Burgers
★☆☆☆☆
Terrible burgers, bad fries.

Puk Yuk Thai
★★★★★
Amazing! Best Thai food in town.

Bangkok House
★☆☆☆☆
Expensive Thai food.

Pierre's French cuisine
★☆☆☆☆
Bad service. Terrible food.

Paris mon amour
★★★★★
Amazing French food.

Make recommendations

9 Writing

Write a short biography

W organizing your notes

A Work in pairs. What can you see in the pictures? What is the connection between them?

B Read the description and complete the notes.

Leonardo da Vinci

Leonardo da Vinci was born near Florence in Italy in 1452. He was an artist, a mathematician, a scientist, a musician and a writer. He is famous for his paintings, but he also designed machines. He painted the famous *Mona Lisa*. He painted this picture in 1503 and it is now in the Louvre Museum in Paris, France. It is a picture of a woman with a beautiful smile.

Name:	*Occupation(s):*
Birth date:	*Why famous?*
Birth place:	*Famous painting:*

Organizing your notes

When you are planning your writing, think about how to organize your notes. In a biography, you can start with personal information (date and place of birth), describe their job, say why they are famous and finally describe one thing they are famous for.

C Read the notes below. Number the information in the best order for a description.

- ☐ artist
- ☐ changed the world of art
- ☐ *1* Pablo Picasso
- ☐ Cubism, new style of painting
- ☐ Málaga, Spain
- ☐ 1881

WRITING

A PLAN Add any more details that you know about Picasso. Decide where to write this information.

B WRITE Write a description using the information in Exercise C. Compare with a partner.

Write a short biography

Unit 9 Review

GRAMMAR

A Complete the sentences with the correct past form of *be*.

1 Shakespeare ________ a writer and a poet.
2 Pablo Picasso and Marie Tussaud ________ artists.
3 **A:** ________ Maya Angelou a poet?
B: Yes, she ________.
4 **A:** ________ Gandhi a scientist?
B: No, he ________.
5 There ________ any phone selfies in the 1700s.
6 There ________ a black president of South Africa before Nelson Mandela.

B Complete the sentences with past tense forms in the positive (+) or negative (-).

1 Last weekend, I ________ (+ *stay*) at home and I ________ (+ *paint*) my bedroom.
2 Tamara ________ (– *pick up*) her computer from the store, but she ________ (+ *organize*) her files.
3 Omar ________ (– *visit*) his grandma, but he ________ (+ *call*) her at home.

VOCABULARY

A Complete the sentences with words for ordinal numbers.

1 We live in the *twenty-first* (*21st*) century.
2 Shakespeare lived in the ________ (*16th*) century.
3 March is the ________ (*3rd*) month of the year.
4 George Washington was the ________ (*1st*) US president.

B Complete the description with the past form of a verb from the box.

be	help	return	start	study	travel

Marco Polo

Marco Polo was born in Venice in 1254. He and his father [1] ________ to China. They [2] ________ their journey in 1271 when Marco Polo [3] ________ 17 years old. The journey was long and difficult. Marco Polo stayed in China for many years and [4] ________ Chinese language and culture. When Marco [5] ________ to Italy 26 years later, his friend [6] ________ him to write a book about his experiences.

10 IT'S HISTORY

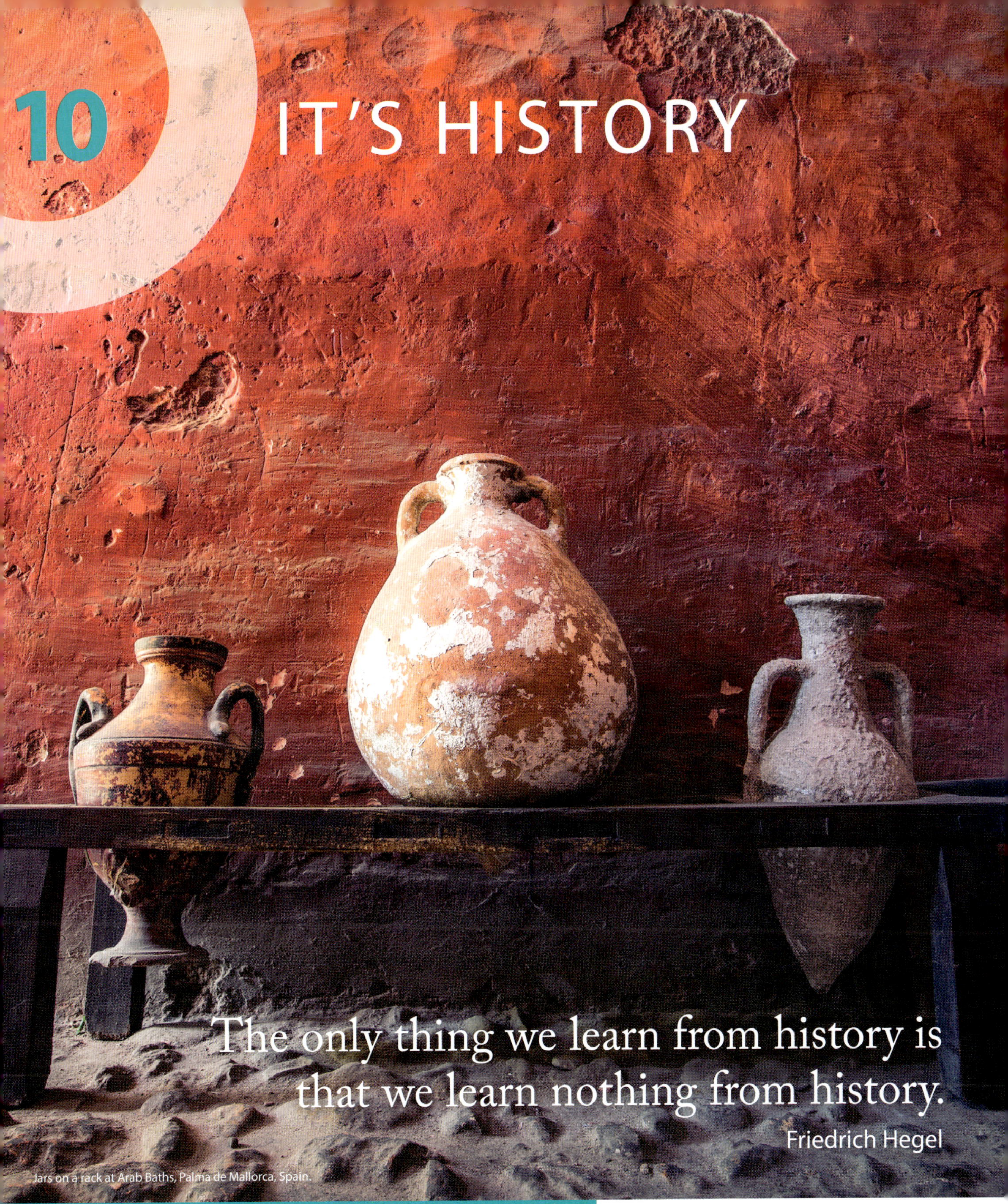

Jars on a rack at Arab Baths, Palma de Mallorca, Spain.

OBJECTIVES

- talk about past events
- talk about past experiences
- talk about what you did on the weekend
- write a paragraph about a past event

Work with a partner. Discuss the questions.

1 Look at the picture. What can you see?

2 Choose words to describe the objects in the picture.

beautiful boring important interesting old new useful

3 Are you interested in history?

10.1 Precious finds

Talk about past events

G simple past: irregular verbs V time phrases P vowel sounds: /ɔː/ and /oʊ/

A HISTORY OF THE WORLD IN 100 OBJECTS

The British Museum in London has a lot of important objects from the past. A few years ago, the museum director started an interesting project. He **chose** 100 objects from the museum to tell a history of the world. Here are just four of the objects. What do they tell us about the past?

HAND AXE

1.2–1.4 million years old, Olduvai Gorge, Tanzania

Scientists **found** many of these hand axes in different regions of Africa. The first humans didn't have metal. They **made** these axes from stone and used them to cut meat and wood.

GOLD MODEL CHARIOT

5th–4th century BCE, Tajikistan

The Persians **built** many new roads across their country. The man in this model **went** from town to town in his chariot. He collected money for the king and carried important messages for people.

TWO-HEADED SNAKE

15th–16th century, Aztec Empire, Mexico

600 years ago, the Aztec people **gave** this bright blue snake to the Aztec Emperor. It **took** a lot of time and skill to make this beautiful object. We think the Emperor **wore** it to show how important he was.

BANKNOTE

CE 135, China

In the 2nd century, Chinese people **bought** and **sold** things using these banknotes. They made banknotes from paper. Before this, people used coins. This banknote was the same as 1,000 coins. The Emperor's name was on these notes to show that they were real.

READING

A PREDICT Look at the pictures above. Which object do you think is most interesting?

B READ FOR GIST Read the introduction to *A history of the world in 100 objects*. Choose the best option to complete the summary.

The museum director chose these objects because …

1 they show us what life was like in the past.
2 they tell us about important events.
3 they belonged to important people.

C READ FOR MAIN IDEA Read the text and match each sentence with an object from the text.

1 This was the first kind of paper money. ______
2 People used this to cut things. ______
3 They made it for an important person. ______
4 This was a way to travel around the country. ______

D SPEAK Work in pairs. Ask and answer questions about each object.

1 Where is it from? 2 How old is it? 3 What is it for?

E SPEAK Work in pairs. Discuss the questions.

1 Which objects are beautiful? Which are useful?
2 Which objects do you use today?

GRAMMAR

Simple past: irregular verbs

A Read *A history of the world in 100 objects* again. Complete the table with words in bold in the article.

Irregular verb	Past form	Irregular verb	Past form
build	1 ______	go	6 ______
buy	2 ______	make	7 ______
choose	3 ______	sell	8 ______
find	4 ______	take	9 ______
give	5 ______	wear	10 ______

B Read the text again. There is one example of the simple past negative. Find and underline it.

C WORK IT OUT Choose the correct options to complete the rules. Use *A history of the world in 100 objects* to help you.

Simple past: irregular verbs

1 Irregular verbs *have* / *don't have* -*ed* in the past.
2 We *add* / *don't add* -*s* to the third person singular in the past.
3 We use *didn't* + verb / verb + -*ed* + *not* in negative sentences.

A lot of common verbs have irregular past tense endings. See the irregular verbs list on page 97.

D Go to the Grammar Hub on page 116.

VOCABULARY
Time phrases

A Read the short text below. Underline time phrases with *in*, *last* and *ago*.

We studied this painting in our art class last year. The artist, Zhang Zeduan, painted this picture 1,000 years ago. It shows everyday life in China in the 12th century.

B Write the time expressions in the table.

the 12th century ~~fifty years~~ 1600 a long time month an hour Friday the past week

Ago	Last	In
fifty years		

C Complete the sentences with *in*, *last* or *ago*.

1 A hundred years ______ people didn't have cell phones.

2 Women wore long dresses ______ the 15th century.

3 People found some old gold coins here ______ year.

D SPEAK Work in pairs. Describe how life was different in the past. Use the topics in the box to help you.

clothes homes money shopping transportation

A: How was life different in the past?
B: People didn't buy clothes in a store very frequently. They made clothes at home.

PRONUNCIATION
Vowel sounds: /ɔː/ and /oʊ/

10.1 **A** Read and listen to the vowel sound in these words. Listen again and repeat.

/ɔː/	bought	saw	tall	walk
/oʊ/	chose	go	nose	phone

10.2 **B** Circle words with the same sound as *bought*. Underline words with the same sound as *chose*. Then listen and check.

floor four know slow show talk toe wore

C SPEAK Work in pairs. Describe five things you did last week. Use the past tense form of the verbs in the box.

buy call choose see talk tell walk

A: I walked to school.
B: I bought some new shoes.

SPEAKING

A PREPARE Work in groups. Choose five objects that explain what life is like in the 21st century and why they are important.

smartphone *talk with friends*
1 ______ ______
2 ______ ______
3 ______ ______
4 ______ ______
5 ______ ______

B PRESENT Imagine you are in the 25th century. Explain what life was like in the 21st century. Use your ideas from Exercise A.

C DISCUSS Work with another group. Can you agree on the five most important objects?

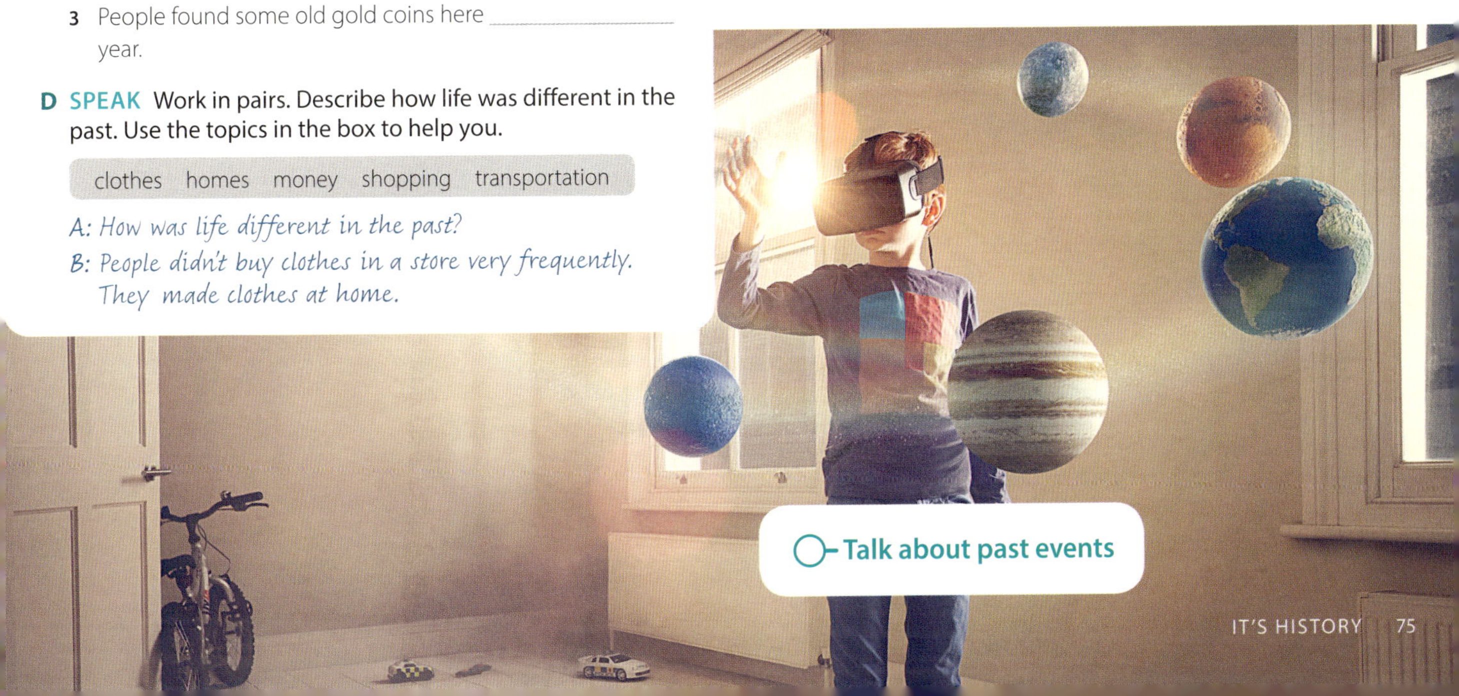

Talk about past events

10.2 Family treasures

Talk about past experiences

V life events S identifying reasons G simple past questions P final consonant /t/ and /d/

VOCABULARY

Life events

A Read the descriptions. Underline the verbs in the simple past.

a This is a picture of me and my girlfriend, Susan. I met her on the first day of college. This is the day we finished college.

b I wrote a short story for the school competition when I was in school and I won first prize!

c This is a picture of me and my husband on the day we got married! It was in the Bahamas – it was really beautiful.

d This is the day I passed my driving test! I was really happy. This sports car belonged to my uncle and I drove it home after the test.

B Match the two parts of each phrase (1–8) with (a–h) to make collocations from Exercise A. Use each verb (1–8) only once.

1 pass	a a person
2 meet	b a story
3 finish	c a car
4 write	d a prize
5 belong	e to someone
6 get	f a test
7 win	g college
8 drive	h married

C SPEAK Describe three important events in your life. Say when they happened.

A: I passed my driving test three years ago.
B: I finished college in 2010.

LISTENING

A PREDICT Look at the pictures. What do you think is the same about all the objects?

B LISTEN FOR GIST 10.3 Listen to three people speaking about the objects. Write the name of the person (Janine, Alfie or Isabel) under the object they talk about.

Identifying reasons

The phrases *that's the reason* or *that's why* come **after** the reason. The reason is in the sentence **before**.

She gave me the camera *That's why* I became a photographer.

C LISTEN FOR DETAIL 10.3 Listen again and complete the table with information from the podcast.

	Object	Who gave it to the speaker?	When did they give it?	Why is it important?
1	*silver pocket watch*			
2				
3				

D SPEAK Tell your partner about an object that is important to you. Did someone give it to you? Did you get it for a special reason?

My parents gave me a necklace on my 18th birthday.

GRAMMAR
Simple past questions

A Read the extracts from the podcast. <u>Underline</u> *did* and the base form of the verbs.

Wh- questions

1 And where did this watch come from originally?
2 What did your great-grandfather use it for?

Yes/No questions

3 **A:** Did your mother take a lot of photos?
B: Yes, she did.
4 **A:** Did you buy this?
B: No, someone gave it to me.

B WORK IT OUT Complete the rules using words from the box. There are some words you do not need.

after before past present *wh-* questions *yes/no* questions

Simple past questions

1 We use *did* to make questions in the simple ______________.
2 Question words (*what, where, when, why* and *how*) come ______________ *did.*
3 We use *did/didn't* in short answers to ______________.

C PRACTICE Reorder the words to write simple past questions.

1 you / a special gift / did / get / on your 21st birthday
______________________________?
2 win / what kind of / you / did / prizes / at school
______________________________?
3 did / your best friend / you / meet / when
______________________________?
4 pass / you / did / tests / any / last year
______________________________?

D Go to the **Grammar Hub** on **page 116**.

E SPEAK Work in pairs. Ask and answer the questions in Exercise C.

PRONUNCIATION
Final consonant /t/ and /d/

10.4 **A** Read and listen to these examples. Notice the final sounds in each pair.

1 mate made
2 right ride
3 hat had

10.5 **B** Listen and choose the word you hear.

1 write / ride
2 wrote / rode
3 sent / send
4 hat / had
5 sat / sad
6 set / said

C Work in pairs. Say one word from each pair in Exercise B. Ask your partner to identify the word.

SPEAKING HUB

A PREPARE Work in groups. Group A – Stay on this page. Group B – Go to the **Communication Hub** on **page 129**. Read the survey. You need to write one person's name for each sentence and find out extra information.

Find someone who:

1 … lived in another country when they were a child.
Where?
2 … passed a test not long ago.
What?
3 … wrote an email yesterday.
Why?
4 … finished college more than five years ago.
Where?

B PLAN Write the questions you need to ask for each item.

Did you live in another country when you were a child?
Where did you live?

C PRACTICE Walk around the classroom and ask questions. Write the names and the answers.

A: Did you live in another country when you were a child?
B: Yes, I did.
A: Where did you live?

D REPORT Work with someone from Group B. Tell them what you found out.

Elsa lived in Brazil when she was young. She lived there for three years and she loved it!

Talk about past experiences

Café Hub

10.3 It was amazing!

F– show interest

COMPREHENSION

A Watch the video. Who had a good weekend? Who had a bad weekend? Who had a good and bad weekend? Check (✓) the boxes.

	Good weekend	Bad weekend
 Carolina	☐	☐
 Onur	☐	☐
 Mark	☐	☐
 Gaby	☐	☐

B Answer the questions. Write the names in the spaces provided.

1 Who went to Paris? ______

2 Who watched the match? ______ ______

3 Who went to the hairdresser's? ______ ______

4 Who went to a concert? ______

5 Who had a pizza? ______

C Watch the video again and check your answers to Exercise B.

Glossary

match (n) (British) = game (n) (American)

FUNCTIONAL LANGUAGE

Showing interest

A Complete the responses to good and bad news with the words in the box.

great love nice Really shame sounds think too

Good news	Bad news
Oh, very [1] ______.	Oh no, that [7] ______ awful.
[2] ______? Wow!	Oh, what a [8] ______.
Cool. I [3] ______ Paris.	
Really? Me, [4] ______.	
Well, that's [5] ______.	
I [6] ______ it's amazing!	

B Circle the correct options (a, b or c) to complete the conversation.

Mark: Onur, what did you do?
Onur: I went to France with some friends.
Mark: Oh, [1] ______. Where did you go?
Onur: We went to Paris.
Mark: Really? [2] ______!
Onur: Yes, it was amazing.
Carolina: [3] ______, I love Paris.
Mark: And what about you, Carolina. How was your weekend?
Carolina: It was also [4] ______. I watched the match on Saturday.
Mark: [5] ______? Me too. Did you enjoy it?
Carolina: Yes, it was [6] ______.
Mark: And Gaby, what did you do this weekend?
Gaby: Well, on Saturday I went to the hairdresser's and it was bad. Then on Sunday I ate a pizza and it was bad.
Carolina: Oh no, that sounds [7] ______.
Gaby: It was.
Mark: Oh. [8] ______.

	a	b	c
1	very nice	bad	awful
2	What a shame	Wow	Oh no
3	Cool	Oh no	What a shame
4	awful	amazing	bad
5	Oh no	Really	That sounds awful
6	great	awful	amazing
7	great	awful	amazing
8	Really	What a shame	Oh no

C Watch the video again and check your answers to Exercises A and B.

GABY

SAM

LUCY

PRONUNCIATION

A Listen to the conversation and notice how the underlined words are stressed. 0.6

Astrid: What did you do on the weekend?
Patrick: I played tennis. It was great.
Astrid: That sounds good.
Patrick: Then I had lunch with my friend.
Astrid: Oh, very nice.
Patrick: But the food was terrible.
Astrid: Oh, what a shame.

B Listen again and repeat the conversation. Copy the stress. 0.6

SPEAKING

A PLAN Imagine you did the activities in the pictures below last weekend. Decide if they were good or bad and say why.

have a picnic

bad, rain

have brunch

amazing, delicious

go to the hairdresser's

go to a party

go to the beach

go ice-skating

B PREPARE Work in pairs. Talk about your weekends. Listen and respond to your partner.

A: On Saturday I ______________. It was ______________.
B: Oh, that sounds *great* / *good* / *bad* / *awful*!

C PRACTICE Go around the class and find out what other people did on the weekend. Listen and respond to what they say.

A: What did you do on the weekend?
B: I went to a birthday party. It was great.
A: Oh, very nice.
B: But then I watched a movie and it was bad.
A: Oh, what a shame.

Show interest

10 Writing

Write a paragraph about a past event

W using sequencing words

A Look at the picture. What is it? Where is it from? How old is it?

B Read the story. What do you think happened next?

About | **Submit** | Contact

Every picture tells a story!
Write a story in 100 words.

A lucky coin

On Saturday morning, Jack got up early and went running in the park. After half an hour, he sat down for a break and he saw something gold under the bench. It was an old gold coin. He picked it up. Then, he put it in his pocket and went home. The next day, on his way to work, he saw a poor man and gave the gold coin to him. A few days later, Jack saw the poor man again. The man walked over to Jack and said, 'I sold the coin for $100 yesterday. Here's $50 for you.'

C Read the story and answer the questions.

1 What did Jack find? ____________

2 Where did he find it? ____________

3 What did he do with it? ____________

4 What happened in the end? ____________

Using sequencing words

Sequencing words, for example *after, then, later,* help the reader to understand the order of events in a story.

D Underline the sequencing words in the story. Put the actions in the order they happened in the story.

☐ Jack sat down for a break.
☐ Jack gave the coin to the poor man.
☐ Jack put the coin in his pocket.
☐ The poor man offered Jack money.
☐ Jack went running.
☐ Jack found a coin.

E Choose the correct options to complete the story. Finish the last line of the story.

Last week, Vicky saw a lamp in the window of an old furniture store. It was very beautiful and she looked at it for a long time. [1]*Then / After*, she went to work. A week [2]*next / later*, she came back to the store, but the lamp wasn't in the window. [3]*Later / After* a couple of minutes, she decided to …

____________.

WRITING

A PLAN Choose one of the story starters and write notes about what happened next.

B WRITE Write the story in 100 words.

- Last summer, we were on vacation in Greece. We walked on the beach every day and one day we found …
- Yesterday morning, Julia went to a market. There were a lot of old paintings. After a few minutes, she saw …
- About three weeks ago, I found a lot of old boxes in my grandparents' garage. I opened one of them and there was …

Write a paragraph about a past event

Unit 10 Review

GRAMMAR

A Complete the sentences in the positive or negative form of the simple past.

1 She ____________ (*buy*) a new watch last Saturday. (-)

2 He ____________ (*drive*) to work on Monday. (+)

3 My father ____________ (*sell*) his car two weeks ago. (+)

4 They ____________ (*find*) the hotel last week. (-)

5 I ____________ (*wear*) a coat yesterday. (-)

6 We ____________ (*give*) her a present for her birthday. (+)

B Complete the conversation with the simple past forms of the verbs in the box.

go see take

Kit: Where [1] ____________ you ____________ last weekend?

Ben: We [2] ____________ to the art museum.

Kit: Really? What [3] ____________ you ____________ there?

Ben: We [4] ____________ some art from Ancient Greece.

Kit: Really? [5] ____________ you ____________ any photos?

Ben: Yes, I did. I [6] ____________ a lot of photos.

VOCABULARY

Complete the sentences with the simple past form of verbs from the box and the correct time expressions.

ago finish give go in (x2) last (x2) meet win

1 We ____________ to Switzerland for our vacation ____________ summer.

2 Sushila ____________ college ____________ 2014.

3 Tony ____________ first prize in the art competition two years ____________.

4 Eliana ____________ her new friend on vacation in Greece ____________ year.

5 They ____________ this watch to my father ____________ 2009.

11 HAVING FUN

Senior man with hands raised, riding a rollercoaster.

OBJECTIVES

- talk about things you like doing
- talk about favorite sports, music and movies
- make and respond to suggestions
- write a personal profile

Work with a partner. Discuss the questions.

1 Look at the picture. How do you think the man feels?
2 Do you like theme parks?
3 Read the quote. Tell each other about things you enjoy.

11.1 In or out?

Talk about things you like doing

V recreational activities   G *like/love/hate/enjoy* + verb + *-ing*   P verb + *-ing* /ŋ/

Is STAYING IN the new GOING OUT?

There are a lot of things you can do to relax on the weekend. You can go to a restaurant or the movie theater. Or you can go to a concert or maybe a soccer game. Did you do any of these things last weekend? For a lot of people, the answer is no. **They don't like going out.** They just want to stay at home. We talked to three people to find out why.

a

b

Why do you like staying in?

Agnes

I love movies. [1] ______________, but I don't like going to the movie theater. I don't like the food they sell there. **I love getting takeout food**, spending time with my family and watching TV and movies at home.

Lee

I'm a soccer fan, [2] ______________. You can watch games from all over the world on TV. My friends come to my house, and we chat and eat snacks, and **we enjoy watching sports together**. It's a great way to spend time with friends.

Frieda

My favorite type of music is rock. [3] ______________, and in my car. **My husband loves going to concerts** and he goes out all the time. But **I hate going to concerts** – they're expensive and there are too many people! **I like staying at home** and listening to my favorite music really loud!

READING

A SPEAK Work in pairs. Ask your partner about last weekend.

A: What did you do last weekend?

B: I went to an Italian restaurant. What about you?

B PREPARE TO READ Read the headline of *Is staying in the new going out?* and look at the pictures. Match the underlined words with the pictures (a and b).

C READ FOR GIST Read the first paragraph of the article. Choose the correct options to complete the summary.

There [1]*are / aren't* a lot of things that people do to relax [2]*in the week / on the weekend*. The article says people these days mostly want to [3]*stay in / go out*.

D READ FOR DETAIL Read the rest of the article. Choose the correct phrase to fill in the blanks in the text.

a I listen to it at home

b I watch them every weekend

c but I don't go to games

E READ FOR SPECIFIC INFORMATION Read the article again and choose the correct options.

1 Agnes doesn't go to the movie theater because …

a it's expensive.

b she doesn't live near a movie theater.

c she doesn't like the food.

2 Lee doesn't go to games because …

a he can watch a lot of sports at home.

b they're expensive.

c he doesn't like the snacks.

3 Frieda doesn't go to concerts because …

a it costs a lot of money.

b she doesn't like music.

c she doesn't like loud music.

F SPEAK Work in pairs. Are you similar to Agnes, Lee or Frieda? Give examples.

VOCABULARY

Recreational activities

A Complete the phrases with the words in the box.

~~family~~	friends	a museum	the park	TV	a video online

1 spend time with *family*

2 go to ______________

3 watch ______________

4 watch ______________

5 spend time with ______________

6 go to ______________

B Go to the Vocabulary Hub on page 126.

C SPEAK Talk to your partner. Ask and answer questions about the recreational activities you like.

A: Do you watch a lot of TV?

B: Yes! I love it! Where do you usually spend time with your friends?

A: At a café, or sometimes at home.

GRAMMAR

like/love/hate/enjoy + verb + *-ing*

A WORK IT OUT Read the phrases in bold in *Is staying in the new going out?* Choose the correct option.

In these phrases, the people are talking about their feelings about *activities* / *objects*.

B Match the words with the emojis.

enjoy hate like love

1 ______ 2 ______ ______ 3 ______

C WORK IT OUT Complete the rules with the words in the box.

negative phrases positive phrases questions

1 In ______, we use *like/love/hate/enjoy* + verb + *-ing*.

2 In ______, we use *do/does* + *not* + *like/love/hate/enjoy* + verb + *-ing*.

3 In ______, we use *do/does* + subject + *like/love/hate/enjoy* + verb + *-ing*.

D Go to the **Grammar Hub** on **page 118**.

PRONUNCIATION

Verb + *-ing* /ŋ/

1.1 **A** Read and listen to the sentence. Choose the correct option to complete the statement.

I like listening to music in the kitchen.

The underlined letters have *the same sound* / *different sounds*.

1.2 **B** Listen and repeat the sentences.

1 He likes going out and spending time with his friends.

2 She likes staying in and watching TV.

11.3 **C** Listen and circle the word you hear.

1 ban / bang 2 thin / thing 3 win / wing

11.4 **D** Listen to the questions. Write the missing words.

1 Do you like *getting* *takeout* food?

2 Do you and your friends like ______ to the same ______?

3 What do you enjoy ______ on the ______?

4 Who do you enjoy ______ ______ with on the weekend?

5 What do you hate ______ on ______?

6 Where do you like ______ out to ______?

E SPEAK Work in pairs. Ask and answer the questions in Exercise D.

A: Do you like getting takeout food?
B: No, I don't. I like going to restaurants.

SPEAKING

A PREPARE Take a class survey about free-time activities. Write three activities from the lesson and add three new activities of your own. Include some 'staying in' activities and some 'going out' activities, too.

Activity	Love	Like/Enjoy	Hate	Extra info
go to the park	✓			*near school*
watch TV				

B PRACTICE Ask other students about the activities they like, enjoy, love and hate.

A: Do you like going to the park?
B: Yes, I love it!
A: Which park do you like?
B: I like the park next to the school.

C REPORT Work in pairs. Look at your results. Answer the questions. Tell the class.

1 What activities do people like, enjoy, love and hate?

2 Do the people in the class like staying in or going out?

Ten people love going to the park. No one hates going to the park.

In general, the people in this class like going out.

Talk about things you like doing

11.2 Super fans

Talk about favorite sports, music and movies

S listening for opinions G object pronouns V entertainment P vowel sounds: /ʊ/ and /uː/

LISTENING

11.5 **A** Look at the picture below. Who is the man, and where is he from? Listen to the radio show interview and check.

11.5 **B** Listen again. Choose the correct options to complete the summary.

They are at a [1]*basketball / soccer* game in the [2]*Olympic / Athletic* Stadium between [3]*England / Germany* and Egypt.
They are waiting to [4]*play / watch* their favorite player, Mo Salah.

Listening for opinions

When we want to give our opinion about something we can use the phrase *I think* to start the sentence. We can also use adjectives, for example *interesting*, *boring*, to show how we feel about something. We use *because* to introduce reasons for our opinion.

I think he's great … I also like him because he's a nice person.

My boyfriend loves soccer, but I hate it – it's so boring.

11.5 **C** Answer the questions. Listen again and check your answers.

1. Who says Mo Salah is number one in the world? *Wendy / Kelly / Ryan*
2. Who says Mo Salah is a nice person? *Wendy / Kelly / Ryan*
3. Who says Mo Salah is good to his fans? *Wendy / Kelly / Ryan*
4. Who doesn't like any other soccer players? *Wendy / Kelly / Ryan*
5. Who isn't interested in soccer at all? *Wendy / Kelly / Ryan*

D SPEAK Work in pairs. Do you like soccer? Why/Why not?

GRAMMAR

Object pronouns

A Read these sentences from the radio show interview. Answer the questions.

Wendy: I'm here to see Mo Salah.
Interviewer: Why do you like him?

1. What or who is the object of Wendy's sentence?
2. Which word does the interviewer use to replace the object of Wendy's sentence?

B Read more sentences from the listening. Underline the object pronouns and circle the people or things they refer to.

1. Kelly: My boyfriend loves soccer, but I hate it.
2. Interviewer: What do you think about Mo Salah?
   Kelly: My boyfriend likes him.
3. Interviewer: So, Ryan, what do you think about the other soccer players?
   Ryan: I'm not interested in them.

C WORK IT OUT Complete the table with the object pronouns in the box.

her him it ~~me~~ them us you (x2)

Subject pronouns	Object pronouns
I play tennis with Luke.	Luke plays tennis with [1] ___me___.
You watch TV with Harry.	Harry watches TV with [2] ______.
He knows a lot of people.	A lot of people know [3] ______.
She plays soccer.	I play soccer with [4] ______.
It is a great movie.	I love watching [5] ______.
We like staying in with Mike.	Mike likes staying in with [6] ______.
You can all come to my house.	I'm happy to see [7] ______ all.
They are musicians.	I like listening to [8] ______.

D Go to the Grammar Hub on page 118.

E SPEAK Complete the sentences with your own ideas. Then complete the questions with the correct object pronoun. Work in pairs and ask and answer the questions.

1. ______ is a famous pop singer in my country. Do you know ______?
2. ______ is the name of a stadium in my town/city. Do you know ______?
3. ______ is a sports (soccer/basketball, etc) team in my country. Do you know ______?

VOCABULARY
Entertainment

A Look at the pictures and read the sentences. Put the words in bold in the correct category.

Rihanna's one of my favorite **pop stars**. I go to all her **concerts**.

The **stadium** is always full when Brazil plays. They're really good **players** and the **games** are usually exciting.

My favorite **movie stars** were at the **movie theater** on Hollywood Boulevard to watch the **premiere**.

People:			
Events:			
Places:			

B Go to the Vocabulary Hub on page 126.

C Choose the correct option to complete the sentences.

1 My favorite ***actor*** / ***player*** is Scarlet Johansson; I have all her movies on DVD.

2 I think Antoine Griezmann is a really good soccer ***player*** / ***singer***.

3 Justin Timberlake was a famous ***pop star*** / ***player*** when I was a teenager.

4 There are many famous pop ***players*** / ***stars*** in my country.

5 My brother's in a ***classical*** / ***rock*** band. He plays the electric guitar.

6 I love watching ***action movies*** / ***comedies***. All of my favorite movies are funny!

D **SPEAK** Work in pairs. Discuss the sentences in Exercise C. Make sentences that are true for you.

My favorite actor is …

PRONUNCIATION
Vowel sounds: /ʊ/ and /uː/

A 11.6 Listen and repeat.

/ʊ/ took, sugar, book   /uː/ two, June, blue

B 11.7 Listen to the sentences. Which sound do the underlined words have?

1 My father is a <u>good</u> <u>cook</u>. /ʊ/ /uː/

2 <u>Moon</u> is my favorite sci-fi movie. I like horror movies, <u>too</u>. /ʊ/ /uː/

C 11.8 Listen and read the sentences. <u>Underline</u> the word that includes the sound in parentheses.

1 The soccer game starts soon. (/uː/)

2 I like cooking Italian food. (/ʊ/)

3 My daughter loves going to school. (/uː/)

4 I know that woman. (/ʊ/)

5 I always go out on Tuesday evening. (/uː/)

6 There are a lot of interesting things to look at in the museum. (/ʊ/)

D **SPEAK** Work in pairs. Make a short sentence that includes one of the words in the box. Say it to your partner. Listen and check your partner's pronunciation.

book foot good look museum the news too Tuesday

I watch the news on TV every evening.

SPEAKING HUB

A **PREPARE** Think about the things that you enjoy doing. Why do you like them? Write some notes.

B **PLAN** You are going to find out if your partner is a superfan. Write some questions. Use the words in the box to help you.

actor movies music player singer sports star

What …? Where …? Who …? Why …?

Do you like watching movies?
What movies do you like watching?
Who is your favorite actor?

C **DISCUSS** Work in pairs. Ask and answer the questions from Exercise B. Is your partner a superfan? Why/Why not?

Talk about favorite sports, music and movies

Café Hub

11.3 Short run

F – make and respond to suggestions

COMPREHENSION

A Watch the video. Underline the correct words or phrases. Then write *Gaby*, *Lucy* or *Both*.

1 *She* / *They* dyed *her* / *their* hair. ______
2 *She's* / *They're* free tomorrow. ______
3 *She wants* / *They want* to go to the gym. ______
4 *She likes* / *They like* breakfast a lot. ______
5 *She's* / *They're* sporty. ______
6 *She says* / *They say* they love running. ______
7 *She doesn't* / *They don't* run far. ______
8 *She has* / *They have* breakfast at Sam's Café. ______

B Correct the information in Gaby's diary. There are five mistakes.

Today	Tomorrow
Wash hair.	Meet Lucy at Newton Green at 9 am.
Call Sam.	Go swimming in the park.
	Go for breakfast at Pizza Roma.

FUNCTIONAL LANGUAGE

Making and responding to suggestions

A 00:18–01:23 Put the telephone conversation in the correct order. Then watch part of the video and check your answers.

a What about going to the gym and then we can have a big breakfast afterwards? ___
b Cool. Do you want to do something? ___
c Sure. Why don't we do something sporty? ___
d No, I'm free all day. 2
e Great, see you there. ___
f OK, how about going for a run and then breakfast? ___
g Yeah, OK. ___
h Perfect. I love running. That sounds really nice. Where do you want to meet? ___
i Er, I'm not sure about the gym, but I like breakfast a lot. ___
j Hi Lucy. Are you busy tomorrow? 1
k Let's meet at Newton Green at eight o'clock tomorrow. ___

B Complete the table with examples from the conversation in Exercise A.

Make a suggestion	Saying yes
What about + verb + *-ing* …	Sure / Great / Perfect
[1] What about going to the gym?	That sounds [5] ______.
How about + verb + *-ing* …	**Saying no**
[2] ______?	I'm not sure about [6] ______.
Why don't we …	**Arrange a place and time**
[3] ______?	Where do you want to meet?
Let's …	Are you busy … + time/day? [7] ______?
[4] ______.	See you there.

GABY

SAM

LUCY

PRONUNCIATION

1.9 **A** Listen to the conversation and notice how the underlined words are stressed.

Charlie: Are you free on Saturday?
Beccie: Yes, I'm free all day.
Charlie: Cool. Do you want to do something?
Beccie: Sure. Why don't we go for a run?
Charlie Uh, I'm not sure about running.
Beccie: OK. How about going for a walk?
Charlie: Great, I love walking. Where do you want to meet?
Beccie: Let's meet at Sam's Café at nine o'clock.
Charlie: Great! See you there.

1.9 **B** Listen again and repeat the conversation. Copy the stress.

SPEAKING

A PLAN Work in pairs.

- Make a list of things you like doing on the weekend.
- Make a list of things you don't like doing on the weekend.

B PREPARE Practice the conversation. Then change roles.

Student A: Suggest something from the list.
Student B: Say no.
Student A: Suggest something from the list.
Student B: Say yes.

C REPEAT Go around the class and make an arrangement with five other students. Use the activities in Exercise A or your own ideas. Complete the table below.

Name	Activity	Place	Time
Sam	Play soccer	The park	5 pm

Make and respond to suggestions

11 Writing

Write a personal profile

W– using *so*

ABOUT ME

Sign up | Login

Helena H.

I'm an artist and a designer, so I love going to museums and art galleries. I have a dog; her name's Kia, and we go on a lot of walks together. I live near the ocean, so we spend a lot of time on the beach. Kia really enjoys running after the birds! I live with my husband and three sons, and they all love football. It's always on TV in our house, and I hate it. I'm not a sports fan at all, so I'm happy to go out for a walk with Kia, or to work on my art.

A Read the text. Join the beginnings (1–4) to the ends (a–d) to make sentences.

1 Helena is
2 She likes
3 She spends time
4 She doesn't like

a going to museums and galleries.
b on the beach with her dog.
c watching sports.
d an artist and a designer.

Using *so*

When we want to talk about a result, we can use *so*.

I'm an artist and a designer, so I love going to museums and art galleries.

I live near the ocean, so we spend a lot of time on the beach.

I'm not a sports fan at all, so I'm happy to go out for a walk.

When we write, we usually put a comma (,) before *so*.

B Use *so* to write short endings to the sentences. Use the ideas in the box to help you.

go to the gym | go shopping | go to the stadium | go to the theater | listen to music at home | spend time in the park

1 I like baseball …
2 I don't enjoy going to concerts …
3 I have three dogs …
4 I love fashion …
5 I enjoy exercise …
6 I'm a fan of Shakespeare …

WRITING

A PLAN You are going to write a personal profile. Write notes about what you like doing and why.

B WRITE Write a short personal profile for the website.

Write a personal profile

Unit 11 Review

GRAMMAR

Find and correct eight mistakes.

WHAT DO YOU LIKE DOING?

Home | Soccer | Basketball | Football | Tennis | Golf | More…

This week: Basketball star Orson Orlando

I'm a professional basketball player, but I don't like watch basketball on TV. I have three children, and I like spend time with they. We enjoying going to the park on the weekend and having fun. My wife is an actor. I love watching she but her doesn't want to watch movies on the weekend. She doesn't liking going to the movie theater, but I love its.

5h | 3

VOCABULARY

Complete the sentences with the words in the box.

actor | basketball | concert | game | premiere | restaurant | singer | takeout

1 Josh Brolin is my favorite __________. I have all his movies on DVD.
2 I don't like cooking. I like staying in and getting __________ food.
3 There's an international soccer __________ on TV tonight.
4 I went to a pop concert last night but I didn't like the __________. He wasn't very good.
5 I went to a movie __________ and I met all the actors. It was really exciting!
6 I like sitting very close to the players when I go to a __________ game.
7 The __________ was very loud but I loved it!
8 I love Chinese food but I don't eat it at home. I like going to the __________ in the town center.

12 GOING AWAY

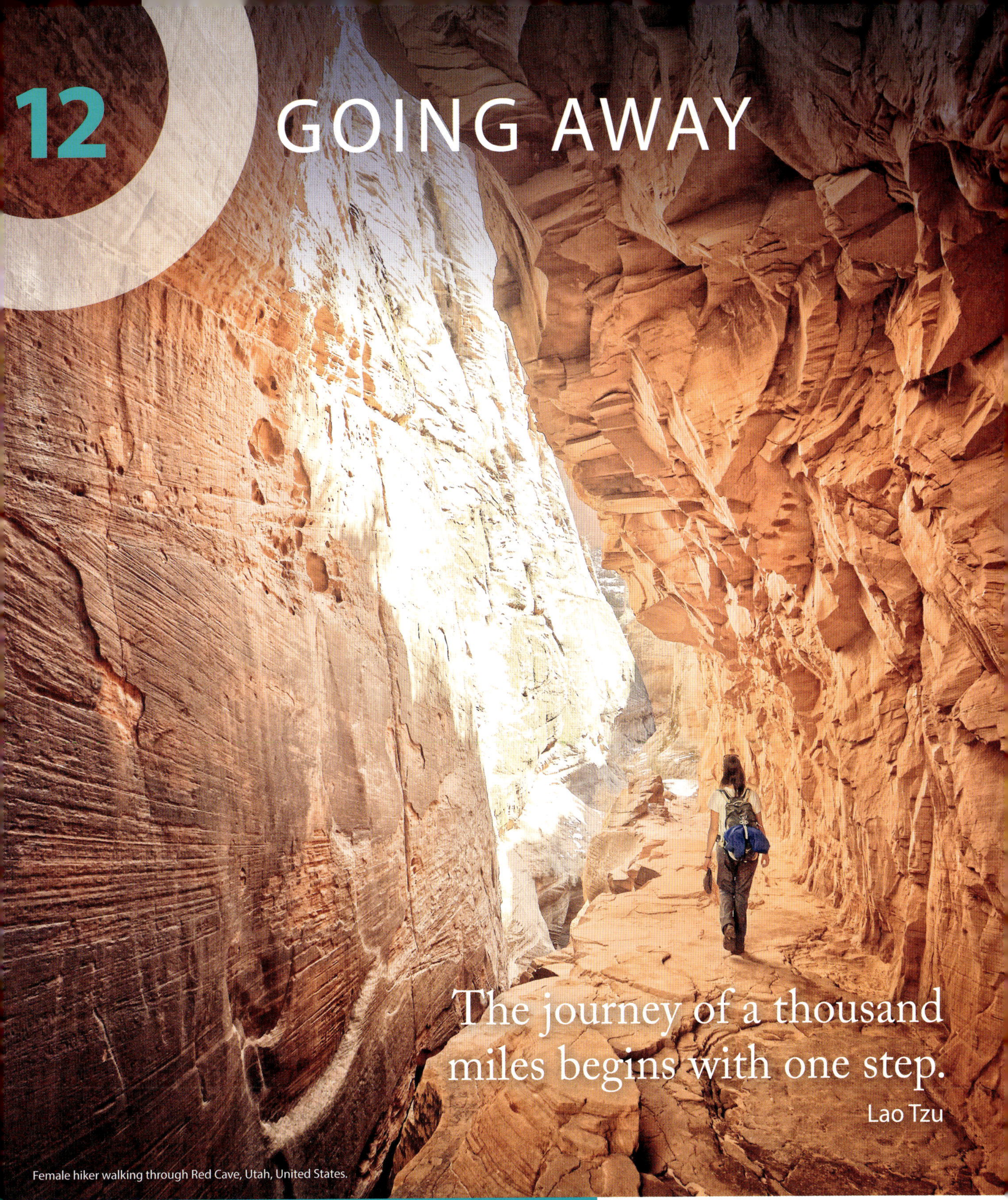

The journey of a thousand miles begins with one step.
Lao Tzu

Female hiker walking through Red Cave, Utah, United States.

OBJECTIVES

- describe a trip
- talk about vacation plans
- ask for and give opinions
- write a postcard

Work with a partner. Discuss the questions.

1 Look at the picture. Do you enjoy long trips?
2 When do you usually go on vacation?
3 What makes long trips difficult?

12.1 Trips

Describe a trip

V travel   **P** consonant clusters   **G** countable and uncountable nouns

READING

A Work in pairs. Make a list of the problems people sometimes have when they travel.

B **READ FOR GIST** Read *A bad trip*. Choose the correct summary.

a Kate McCallister didn't take her son when she went on vacation. She tried to get home, but she had a very bad trip.

b Kate McCallister didn't take her passport when she went on vacation. She went home with her son.

C **READ FOR DETAIL** Put the events (a–e) in the order they happened (1–5). Read the article again to check your answers.

a Kate got on a plane to Paris. ____
b Kate remembered Kevin was at home. ____
c Kate went to Chicago in a van. ____
d Kate went to the airport in Chicago. ____
e Kate got on a plane to Pennsylvania. ____

D **SPEAK** Work in pairs. Answer the questions.

1 Do you ever go on a plane or a train?
2 Do you sometimes forget things when you travel?

A BAD TRIP

A lot can go wrong when you travel. For example:

- Your train to the **airport** is late, so you miss your plane.
- You take a taxi to the airport, but there is a lot of **traffic**, so you miss your plane.
- You forget your **passport**.
- Your **luggage** is too big to take on the plane.
- You forget the **bag** with all of your **money**, your **credit card** and your **ticket** in it.

These are all things that can happen, but I think the worst thing is what happened to Kate McCallister in the 1990 movie *Home Alone*. She went to Paris on vacation with her family. At first, she didn't have any problems. She got to the airport on time, she didn't forget her passport, her luggage wasn't too big, and she had all her bags and all her money with her. She also had all of her credit cards and tickets. But she forgot one very important thing.

When she was on the plane from Chicago to Paris, Kate remembered: her 8-year-old son, Kevin! Kevin was not with them. He was at home … alone!

When they got to Paris, there weren't any planes back to Chicago, so she took a plane to Pennsylvania in the United States. Then, Kate tried to get a plane from Pennsylvania to Chicago but there weren't any. So, she traveled home in a van with a traveling group of musicians. Did she get back to Kevin? Was he okay? Watch the movie to find out!

VOCABULARY

Travel

A Match the images with the words in bold in the article.

1 ____________

5 ____________

2 ____________

6 ____________

3 ____________

7 ____________

4 ____________

8 ____________

B Go the the Vocabulary Hub on page 127.

C Choose the correct options to complete the conversation.

Leo: Do you have your [1]*passport* / *taxi*? You need it to get on the [2]*plane* / *airport*.

Mia: Yes, I do. It's in my bag.

Leo: Do you have some [3]*money* / *luggage*? We need to exchange it at the airport for [4]*dollars* / *tickets*.

Mia: Yes, I do. It's in my bag.

Leo: Do you have the [5]*tickets* / *credit cards* for the train to the [6]*airport* / *station*?

Mia: Yes, I do. They're in my bag.

Leo: Do you have your bag?

Mia: Yes, I ... Oh wait. No, I don't. I think it's at home.

PRONUNCIATION

Consonant clusters

2.1 A Listen to the sentences. Notice how we say the underlined letters.

You need your ticket to get on the plane.

I took a train at the station.

2.2 B Listen to the words. Underline the consonant clusters.

blue class fly plane travel

2.3 C Listen and circle the words you hear.

1 rain / train
2 tea / tree
3 top / stop
4 red / bread
5 back / black

GRAMMAR

Countable and uncountable nouns

A Read the sentences from the article. What do you notice about the words in bold? Are they talking about one bag, or more than one?

1 You forget the **bag** that has your money, your credit card and your ticket in it.
2 ... her luggage wasn't too big, and she had all her **bags** and all her money with her.

B What do you notice about the underlined words?

C WORK IT OUT Choose the correct option to complete the sentences.

Countable and uncountable nouns

1 *Bag* / *Money* is a countable noun: it has a singular and a plural form.
2 *Bag* / *Money* is an uncountable noun: it doesn't have a plural form.

D PRACTICE Choose the correct options. Use examples from the article *A bad trip* to help you.

1 *all of your monies* / *all of your money*
Money is a(n) *countable* / *uncountable* noun.
2 *all of her credit cards* / *all of her credit card*
Credit card is a(n) *countable* / *uncountable* noun.
3 *her luggages* / *her luggage*
Luggage is a(n) *countable* / *uncountable* noun.
4 *a lot of traffic* / *a lot of traffics*
Traffic is a(n) *countable* / *uncountable* noun.

E Go to the Grammar Hub on page 120.

SPEAKING

A PREPARE Work in pairs. Read the description of a trip. Answer the questions.

I took a train from New York to Philadelphia. The train left on time but soon after we got to Pennsylvania the train stopped. There was a tree on the track and the train couldn't move! In the end, we got on a bus. We arrived in Philadelphia two hours late.

1 Where did she start?
2 Where did she finish?
3 How did she travel?
4 What was the problem?

B PLAN Think about a bad trip you went on. Prepare the answers to these questions.

1 Where did you start?
2 Where did you finish?
3 How did you travel?
4 What was the problem?

C DISCUSS Work in groups. Tell each other about your bad trips. Listen and ask questions.

And then what happened?
What did you do?
What happened next?
Oh wow, how did you ...?

Describe a trip

12.2 A prize vacation

Talk about vacation plans

S listening for feelings · V types of vacations · G present progressive · P vowel sounds: /ɪ/, /iː/ and /aɪ/

LISTENING

A SPEAK Work in pairs. Talk about your last vacation. Where did you go? What did you do?

A: I went to Lake Como in Italy. I went hiking, and I ate a lot of great Italian food.
B: For my last vacation, I didn't go away, but I didn't go to work – I just relaxed at home. It was great!

B PREPARE TO LISTEN Read the web page. Answer the questions.

Home | Listen live | Schedule   Search

HUB LIVE – ONLINE RADIO

Mikey Greene's afternoon show

In this week's competition, you can win a vacation for you and a friend.
Enter online. We will call the winner live on the radio. Listen to Tuesday's show and have your phone with you.

1 What is HUB Live?
   a a radio station
   b a TV station
   c a news website
2 Who is Mikey Greene?
   a a vacation expert
   b a singer
   c a radio presenter
3 What is the prize?
   a a radio
   b a vacation
   c a phone
4 How does a listener know they are the winner?
   a They get a phone call on Tuesday.
   b They look online.
   c They get an email on Tuesday.

12.4 **C LISTEN FOR GIST** Listen to the conversation. Choose the picture (a, b, c or d) that shows the vacation. Is the winner happy?

12.4 **D LISTEN FOR DETAIL** Listen again. Answer the questions.

1 What's the name of the competition winner?
2 What's the name of the competition winner's friend?
3 On what day of the week does the vacation start?
4 In which month does the vacation start?
5 How long is the vacation?

Listening for feelings

How we say things can tell the listener how we're feeling. When we're unhappy about something, we usually pause.
Jo: … No beach?
When we're angry or surprised, we usually speak loudly.
Jo: TWO WEEKS?

12.5 **E LISTEN FOR FEELINGS** Listen to Mikey and Jo. Match Jo's words (1–2) with the actions (a–b). What do they tell us about her feelings?

1 Camping. In a tent?   a loud
2 Mountains?   b pause

F SPEAK Work in pairs. Role-play the conversation when the winner tells her friend about the vacation.

A: Hi. I won a vacation for you and me.
B: That's great! Where is it?
A: Uh …

G SPEAK Work in pairs. Imagine you won this vacation. How do you feel?

a

b

c

d

VOCABULARY
Types of vacations

A Match two words or phrases with each of the pictures (a–d) on page 92.

a beach vacation   a camping vacation   a chalet   the ocean   a sightseeing vacation   a skiing vacation   a tent   tourists

B Go to the **Vocabulary Hub** on **page 127**.

C ~~Cross out~~ the option that is not correct.

When you go on vacation, you can …

1 stay in a *tent* / *hotel* / *beach* / *chalet*.
2 take your *sunglasses* / *camera* / *skiing* / *snorkel*.
3 use a *guidebook* / *stove* / *sightseeing* / *camera*.

D Choose the correct option to complete the sentences.

1 We usually go *in* / *on* a beach vacation in August.
2 You can see the ocean *from* / *to* our hotel window.
3 We went sightseeing *around* / *of* Kyoto in Japan.
4 We usually go skiing *in* / *at* the mountains in January.
5 I enjoy camping *with* / *for* my friends.
6 I take a lot of photos *by* / *with* this camera.

E **SPEAK** Work in pairs. Discuss the questions.

1 What is your favorite type of vacation? Why?
2 How often do you go on this type of vacation?
3 What things do you take?

PRONUNCIATION
Vowel sounds:/ɪ/, /iː/ and /aɪ/

2.6 **A** Read and listen to the examples.

/ɪ/	/iː/	/aɪ/
sit	green	why
a	b	c

2.7 **B** Read and listen to the examples from the radio show. Then put the words (1–3) in the correct place in the table.

No [1]beach? Well, you're a [2]winner today. Have a great [3]time.

2.8 **C** Join the first half of the sentences (1–3) to the second half of the sentences (a–c) with underlined letters that have the same sound. Then, listen and check.

1 /ɪ/ This is — a a week at the ski resort.
2 /aɪ/ My prize was — b an interesting vacation.
3 /iː/ He enjoyed — c a guidebook.

D Choose the correct sound for each underlined word.

1 Do you like beach vacations? /ɪ/ /iː/ /aɪ/
2 Do you frequently win competitions? /ɪ/ /iː/ /aɪ/
3 Do you like Jo's prize? /ɪ/ /iː/ /aɪ/

E **SPEAK** Work in pairs. Ask and answer the questions in Exercise D.

GRAMMAR
Present progressive

A **WORK IT OUT** Read the sentences from the radio show. Choose the correct option to complete the rules.

Mikey: **You're going** … next Wednesday!

Mikey: **You're going** to the countryside, and **you're staying** in a tent, next to some mountains.

Present progressive

1 He is talking about an arrangement in the *present* / *future*.
2 He is talking about something that *is* / *isn't* fixed.

B Read the **audio script** on **page 137**. Find six more sentences or questions when Mikey and Jo use present progressive.

C Go to the **Grammar Hub** on **page 120**.

SPEAKING HUB

A **PREPARE** You are going to role-play a conversation between a radio presenter and a prize winner. Work in pairs. Choose roles.

Student A – You are the prize winner. Go to the **Communication Hub** on **page 133**.

Student B – You are the radio presenter. Go to the **Communication Hub** on **page 129**.

B **PRACTICE** Role-play the conversation with your partner.

C **DISCUSS** Have a conversation with your partner. Imagine and plan a vacation you both want to go on. Think about:

- the type of vacation
- the place
- when to go
- where to stay
- how long to go for
- things to take

D **REPORT** Tell the class about your vacation.

We're going on a beach vacation!

Talk about vacation plans

Café Hub

12.3 Istanbul

F – ask for and give opinions

COMPREHENSION

A ▶ 00:10–00:40 Watch the first part of the video. What do you think Lucy's idea is? Choose a, b or c.

a Why don't you come with me to Madrid?
b Let's go on a city break!
c How about going to see Metal Train tonight?

B ▶ 00:41–03:04 Watch the second part of the video and check your answer to Exercise A.

C Match Sam's comments (1–4) with the different places (a–d).

1 It's too rainy. _______
2 It's really expensive. _______
3 It's too busy. _______
4 It's really cold there right now. _______

a Copenhagen

b Helsinki

c Venice

d Dublin

D ▶ Watch the video again and check your answers to Exercise C.

E **SPEAK** Work in pairs. Answer the questions.

1 Which cities in the video would you like to visit?
2 Which cities in your country are like descriptions 1–4 in Exercise C?
3 Which city in the world would you most like to visit?

FUNCTIONAL LANGUAGE

Asking for and giving opinions

A Complete the phrases in the table with the words in the box.

about busy ~~going~~ Good How No really think

Ask for an opinion	Agree
What about [1] *going* on a city break? What [2] _______ Dublin? [3] _______ about Istanbul?	That's a great/nice idea. Perfect! **Disagree** [4] _______ way!
Give an opinion	**Agree**
I think it's [5] _______ expensive. It's really cold there right now. It's too [6] _______ with long queues everywhere. It's too rainy.	Oh yeah. [7] _______ point. That's true. **Disagree** I don't [8] _______ it's *that* cold/busy/rainy etc.

B ▶ Watch the video again and check your answers to Exercise A.

Glossary

city break (n) (British) = a getaway in the city (n) (American)
queues (n) (British) = lines (n) (American)

GABY

SAM

LUCY

PRONUNCIATION

A Listen to the conversation and notice how the underlined words are stressed.

2.9

Michael:	I have a cool idea. Let's go on a getaway.
David:	A weekend away? Together? But where?
Michael:	How about Paris?
David:	I think Paris is very expensive.
Michael:	Good point.-
David:	What about San Sebastián?
Michael:	No way, it's too rainy.
David:	I don't think it's that rainy!
Michael:	But, at this time of year, it rains a lot.
David:	That's true.
Michael:	OK, how about Amsterdam?
David:	Perfect!

B Listen again and repeat the conversation. Copy the stress.

2.9

SPEAKING

A PREPARE Work in pairs. List good and bad points about the cities below.

B PRACTICE Work in pairs. Write and practice a conversation using your ideas from Exercise A.

- Student A: Suggest a city for a getaway.
- Student B: Disagree with Student A three times and explain why.
- Finish the dialogue when Student B agrees with Student A.

C PRESENT Perform your conversation for the other students in the class.

D DISCUSS Find out which is the most popular city in your class.

Rome, Italy

Reykjavík, Iceland

San Francisco, US

Prague, Czech Republic

Dubai, United Arab Emirates

Ask for and give opinions

12 Writing

Write a postcard

W editing your writing

A Read the postcard. Find:

1 the type of vacation ____________
2 the place ____________
3 a useful item ____________
4 a place to visit ____________
5 the first day of the vacation ____________
6 the last day of the vacation ____________

Hi Juan,

I'm on vacation in Casablanca. There are a lot of people, and it's very hot, but I love it! Every day, I go sightseeing. There are some great markets, and I really liked the Hassan II Mosque. It's beautiful. I have a new camera, and I'm taking a lot of photos. I got here last Thursday, and I'm going home tomorrow but I don't want to leave! See you soon.

Kyra

Editing your writing

When you write something, it's a good idea to check for any spelling, grammar or punctuation mistakes.

Im on Vaccation at paris ✗

I'm on ***vacation in*** *Paris.* ✓

B Find and correct the mistakes in this postcard text.

hi Ellie.

Im on vacation in peru. I lov it here! We went to Machu Picchu yesterday. It was beautiful? Tomorrow we going to Lake Titicaca. I can't wate!

See you when I get back,

wendy

WRITING

A PLAN Plan a postcard. Follow the instructions.

- Choose a place to write about.
- Write notes for each of the categories in Exercise A.

B WRITE Imagine you are on vacation now. Write a postcard. Use all of the information you prepared in Exercise A.

C EDIT Check your postcard for mistakes. Think about spelling, grammar and punctuation.

Write a postcard

Unit 12 Review

GRAMMAR

A Choose the correct options to complete the sentences.

1 I have some *moneys* / *money* in my bag.
2 Can I have two *ticket* / *tickets* to Buenos Aires, please?
3 I asked the staff for more *information* / *informations* about the trip.
4 My friend Anna goes on a lot of *vacation* / *vacations*.
5 I don't have any *credit card* / *credit cards*, but I have some cash.
6 Our taxi was late because there was a lot of *traffics* / *traffic*.

B Complete the conversation with the verbs in the box in the present progressive.

drive go take visit be

Sam: Where [1] ____________ you ____________ on vacation this year?
Tom: I [2] ____________ my brother in Virginia.
Sam: [3] ____________ you ____________ the train?
Tom: No, I [4] ____________. I [5] ____________ there.

VOCABULARY

Match the words with the descriptions. Use each word only once.

airport chalet guidebook passport skiing snorkel taxi tent

1 a type of vacation, usually in the mountains ____________
2 a type of transportation ____________
3 something you need when you go to another country ____________
4 a place you can stay in when you are on a skiing vacation ____________
5 something tourists use when they are sightseeing ____________
6 a place where you can get on a plane ____________
7 something you stay in when you are camping ____________
8 something you can use when you are on a beach vacation ____________

Irregular Verbs

Base form	Simple past	Past participle
be	was/were	been
become	became	become
begin	began	begun
break	broke	broken
bring	brought	brought
build	built	built
buy	bought	bought
can	could	(been able to)
catch	caught	caught
choose	chose	chosen
come	came	come
cost	cost	cost
cut	cut	cut
do	did	done
drink	drank	drunk
eat	ate	eaten
fall	fell	fallen
feel	felt	felt
find	found	found
forget	forgot	forgotten
get	got	got
give	gave	given
go	went	gone/been
grow	grew	grown
have	had	had
hear	heard	heard
hit	hit	hit
hold	held	held
hurt	hurt	hurt
keep	kept	kept
know	knew	known
leave	left	left
lend	lent	lent

Base form	Simple past	Past participle
let	let	let
lose	lost	lost
make	made	made
mean	meant	meant
meet	met	met
must	had to	(had to)
pay	paid	paid
put	put	put
read	read	read
ride	rode	ridden
run	ran	run
say	said	said
see	saw	seen
sell	sold	sold
set	set	set
shut	shut	shut
sing	sang	sung
sit	sat	sat
sleep	slept	slept
speak	spoke	spoken
spell	spelled	spelled
spend	spent	spent
stand	stood	stood
steal	stole	stolen
take	took	taken
teach	taught	taught
tell	told	told
think	thought	thought
throw	threw	thrown
understand	understood	understood
wear	wore	worn
win	won	won
write	wrote	written

PHONETIC SYMBOLS											
Single vowels			Diphthongs			Consonants					
/ɪ/	fish	/fɪʃ/	/uw/	new	/nuw/	/p/	pen	/pen/	/s/	snake	/sneɪk/
/iː/	bean	/biːn/	/eɪ/	face	/feɪs/	/b/	bag	/bæg/	/z/	zoo	/zuː/
/ʊ/	foot	/fʊt/	/ɔɪ/	boy	/bɔɪ/	/t/	tea	/tiː/	/ʃ/	shop	/ʃɒp/
/uː/	shoe	/ʃuː/	/oʊ/	nose	/noʊz/	/d/	dog	/dɒg/	/ʒ/	television	/'telɪvɪʒən/
/e/	egg	/eg/	/ju/	use	/juz/	/ʧ/	chip	/ʧɪp/	/m/	map	/mæp/
/ə/	mother	/'mʌðər/	/aɪ/	eye	/aɪ/	/ʤ/	jazz	/ʤæz/	/n/	name	/neɪm/
/ɜː/	word	/wɜːrd/	/aʊ/	mouth	/maʊθ/	/k/	cake	/keɪk/	/ŋ/	ring	/rɪŋ/
/ɔː/	talk	/tɔːk/				/g/	girl	/gɜːrl/	/h/	house	/haʊs/
/æ/	back	/bæk/				/f/	film	/fɪlm/	/l/	leg	/leg/
/ʌ/	bus	/bʌs/				/v/	verb	/vɜːrb/	/r/	road	/roʊd/
/ɑː/	arm	/ɑːrm/				/θ/	thing	/θɪŋ/	/w/	want	/wɒnt/
/ɒ/	top	/tɒp/				/ð/	these	/ðiːz/	/j/	yes	/jes/

Grammar Hub

1.1

Simple present *be*: *I, you*

	Positive	Negative
I	**I am** from Germany.	**I am not** from Germany.
	I'm from Germany.	**I'm not** from Germany.
you	**You are** from Canada.	**You are not** from Canada.
	You're from Canada.	**You aren't** from Canada.
		You're not from Canada.

	Yes/No questions	Short answers
you	**Are you** from Argentina?	**Yes, I am.**
		No, I'm not.

- For the verb *be*, we use *am* with *I* and *are* with *you*.

  I am happy.
  You are happy.
- We can use the long form (*I am / You are*) or the contraction (*I'm/You're*). We typically use the contraction when we speak.

  I am from London. OR I'm from London.
  You are from France. OR You're from France.

Be careful!

- Remember: I am = I'm, You are = You're.

  I'm from Peru. NOT ~~I'm am from Peru.~~
  You're from Brazil. NOT ~~You're are from Brazil.~~

1.2

Simple present *be*: *he, she, it*

	Positive	Negative
he/she/it	**He/She is** a teacher.	**He/She is not** a teacher.
	He's/She's a teacher.	**He/She isn't** a teacher.
		He's/She's not a teacher.
	It is small.	**It is not** small.
	It's small.	**It isn't** small.
		It's not small.

	Yes/No questions	Short answers
he/she/it	**Is he** friendly?	**Yes, he is. / No, he isn't.**
	Is she the manager?	**Yes, she is. / No, she isn't.**
	Is it fun?	**Yes, it is. / No, it isn't.**

- For the verb *be*, we use *is* with *he, she* and *it*.

  He is nice.
  She is nice.
  It is nice.
- We can use the long form (*He is / She is / It is*) or the contraction (*He's / She's / It's*). We typically use the contraction when we speak.

  He is busy. OR He's busy.
  She is happy at her job. OR She's happy at her job.
  It is a big company. OR It's a big company.

Be careful!

- For negative short answers, we usually use the contraction.

  No, she isn't. NOT ~~No, she is not.~~

1.1

Simple present *be*: *I, you*

A Choose the correct options.

1 I *am* / *are* from Madrid.
2 *You're* / *You're are* from Sweden.
3 *I not* / *I'm not* from Berlin.
4 You *not* / *aren't* from Hungary.
5 *You are* / *Are you* from New York?
6 I *are* / *am* from Germany.
7 You *are* / *am* from the UK.
8 *Am* / *Are* you from Indonesia?

B Write the negatives. Use contractions.

1 I'm from Italy.
I'm not from Italy.
2 You're from Brazil.
______
3 I'm from China.
______
4 You're from Egypt.
______
5 I'm from Japan.
______
6 You're from Turkey.
______
7 I'm from Mexico.
______
8 You're from Australia.
______

C Complete the conversations with the words in the box.

am ~~are~~ I I'm no not yes you

1 **A:** ___*Are*___ you from Italy?
B: Yes, I am.
2 **A:** Hello. Are you from Brazil?
B: Yes, I ______.
3 **A:** Are ______ from Australia?
B: Yes, I am.
4 **A:** Are you from Morocco?
B: ______, I am.
5 **A:** Are you from Canada?
B: ______, I'm not.
6 **A:** Good morning. Are you from Argentina?
B: Yes, ______ am.
7 **A:** Hello Lisa. Are you from China?
B: No, I'm ______.
8 **A:** Are you from Mexico?
B: No, ______ not.

➤ Go back to page 3.

1.2

Simple present *be*: *he, she, it*

A Choose the correct options.

1 He ___ an architect.
a be b is
2 My friend is ___ a doctor.
a not b isn't
3 Maria is a manager. ___ very nice.
a It's b She's
4 I like my job. ___ fun.
a It's b She's
5 Paul isn't a teacher. ___ a student.
a He's b It's
6 Her name ___ Karen and she's from Canada.
a is b are

B Complete the email with the words in the box.

he's is (x4) ~~isn't~~ it's she's

Hi Tina!

I'm at work but I'm not very busy. My manager [1] ___*isn't*___ here today because she [2] ______ in New York City. Her name [3] ______ Sandra and [4] ______ very nice. The job [5] ______ fun and I'm very happy here. Henri [6] ______ my colleague. [7] ______ very friendly. We're on the design team. [8] ______ a small team with four people.

See you soon!

Love,

Annette

C Write the correct short answers.

1 **A:** Is Marco a manager?
B: *No, he isn't.* (-)
2 **A:** Is your job difficult?
B: ______ (-)
3 **A:** Is Peter a student?
B: ______ (+)
4 **A:** Is Tina a teacher?
B: ______ (-)
5 **A:** Is your job fun?
B: ______ (+)

➤ Go back to page 5.

Grammar Hub

2.1

Simple present *be*: *we*, *you*, *they*

	Positive	Negative
we	**We are** from New York. **We're** from New York.	**We are not** from Canada. **We aren't** from Canada. **We're not** from Canada.
you	**You are** from Italy. **You're** from Italy.	**You are not** Spanish. **You aren't** Spanish. **You're not** Spanish.
they	**They are** Norwegian. **They're** Norwegian.	**They are not** from Sweden. **They aren't** from Sweden. **They're not** from Sweden.

	Yes/No questions	Short answers
we	**Are we** a great band?	**Yes, you are. / No, you aren't. / No, you're not.**
you	**Are you** musicians?	**Yes, we are. / No, we aren't. / No, we're not.**
they	**Are they** fans of world music?	**Yes, they are. / No, they aren't. / No, they're not.**

- For the verb *be*, we use *are* after the pronouns *we*, *you* and *they*.

  We are from Senegal. We're from Senegal.
  They aren't in a band.
- In *yes/no* questions, the verb *be* is first.

  Are they good at music?
  Are we at the concert?
- The answer to a *yes/no* question is *yes* or *no*, followed by a pronoun and the verb *be*.

  Are you from America? Yes, we are. / No, we aren't. / No, we're not.
  Are they singers? Yes, they are. / No, they aren't. / No, they're not.
- In *yes/no* questions with *no* answers, we can write the contraction in two ways.

  Are they from Boston? No, they aren't. OR No, they're not.

Be careful!

- In *yes/no* questions with *yes* answers, we cannot write the contraction.

  Are you fans of the band? Yes, we are.
  NOT ~~Yes, we're.~~

Possessive adjectives

Subject pronoun	Possessive adjective
I am a fan of American music.	**My** playlist is very cool.
You are from Japan.	**Your** country is in Asia.
He is Malian.	**His** country is in Africa.
We are from France.	**Our** country is in Europe.
They are singers.	**Their** songs are really good.

- For possessive adjectives, we change the subject pronoun to the correct possessive adjective.

  *I'm in a band. **My** band's name is Full Energy.*
  *We are from Poland. **Our** country is quite big.*

2.2

Wh-* questions with *be

Question word	*be*	Rest of question	Answer
What	**is**	your name?	**My name is** Lee.
Where	**are**	you from?	**I am** from China.
Who	**is**	your teacher?	**Our teacher is** Ms. Daniels.
When	**is**	your class?	**It's at** 10 am.
How old	**are**	your friends?	**They are** 14 years old.

- In *wh-* questions, the question word is first.

  What are their jobs?
  Where am I right now?
- In *wh-* questions, the verb is second.

  Who is your classmate?
  Where are Jason and Alex?

Be careful!

- In *wh-* questions, the verb matches the noun after it. The noun is the subject of the *wh-* question.

  Where is their house? NOT ~~Where are their house?~~
  What are your names? NOT ~~What is your names?~~

2.1

Simple present *be*: *we, you, they*; possessive adjectives

A Choose the correct options.

1 Niko and John are Greek. *They* / *We* are from Greece.
2 My best friend and I are Icelandic. *You* / *We* are from Iceland.
3 *You are* / *Are you* from Portugal?
4 Are you fans of his music? Yes, *I* / *we* are.
5 Are your friends from Chile? Yes, *we* / *they* are.
6 Are they free tonight? *No, they're not.* / *Yes, they're.*
7 I'm a fan of music. *My* / *Your* playlist is full of songs.
8 We're from Italy. *Our* / *Their* country is in southern Europe.

B Put the words in the correct order to make sentences and questions.

1 from / your friends / are / Jamaica
Are your friends from Jamaica ?
2 fans / we / of / her / music / aren't
______.
3 great / their / are / songs
______?
4 from / are / they / Reykjavik
______?
5 are / you / favorite / my / singer
______!
6 big fans / new album / they're / their / of
______.
7 classmates / are / Italian / your
______?
8 from / they're / Turkey / not
______.

C Choose the correct options to complete the conversation.

Samantha: Hi, I'm Samantha. [1] ___ in my music class?
Henry: Hi, Samantha. I'm Henry. Yes, [2] ___ in the class together.
Samantha: Great! [3] ___ a big fan of music like me?
Henry: Oh, yes. [4] ___ playlist is full of great songs.
Samantha: That's nice. [5] ___ teacher is really nice, too.
Henry: Yes, I'm excited about [6] ___ lessons.
Samantha: Well, see you in class!
Henry: Bye!

1 **a** Are you **b** You are
2 **a** we're **b** are we
3 **a** You're **b** Are you
4 **a** Your **b** My
5 **a** Our **b** His
6 **a** your **b** my

➤ Go back to page 11.

2.2

Wh-* questions with *be

A Choose the correct options.

1 What ___ your name?
a is **b** are
2 Who ___ your best friends?
a is **b** are
3 Where ___ your teacher from?
a is **b** are
4 How old ___ your parents?
a is **b** are
5 ___ your favorite artist?
a What's **b** Who's
6 ___ your favorite song?
a Where's **b** What's

B Write the correct form of the verb *be* to complete the questions.

1 Where ___are___ Tom and Joseph?
2 What ______ her nationality?
3 Who ______ your favorite musicians?
4 How old ______ Shannon and Michael?
5 What ______ his favorite apps?
6 Who ______ Ariana Grande?
7 How old ______ this movie?
8 When ______ your class?

C Match the questions (1–8) and the answers (a–h).

1 Where are Zara and Aliyah from? _g_
2 Who's your Japanese teacher? ___
3 What's your favorite language? ___
4 How old is your new classmate? ___
5 Where's Karen from? ___
6 How old are your sisters? ___
7 Who are your neighbors? ___
8 When's your class? ___

a It's on Wednesday.
b He's 14.
c They're Mr. and Mrs. Neilson.
d She's from Sweden.
e It's Chinese.
f Mr. Watanabe.
g They're from Egypt.
h They're 24 and 28.

➤ Go back to page 13.

Grammar Hub

3.1

a/an* and plural nouns; *this, that, these, those

a/an	Plural nouns
a hat	three hat**s**
a phone	phone**s**
a box	two box**es**
a baby	three bab**ies**
an umbrella	two umbrella**s**

- We use *a* or *an* to talk about one object.
- We use *an* when the noun starts with a vowel sound (*a, e, i, o, u*). We use *a* when the noun doesn't start with a vowel sound.
- We don't use *a* or *an* with plural nouns (= more than one object).
- We add *-s* to the end of most nouns to make them plural.
- We add *-es* to the end of nouns ending in *-ch* (e.g. *watch – watches*), *-s* or *-ss* (e.g. *class – classes*), *-sh* (e.g. *brush – brushes*), *-x* (e.g. *box – boxes*), and *-o* (e.g. *potato – potatoes*) to make them plural.
- For nouns ending in *-y*, we change the *-y* to *-i-* and add *-es* (e.g. *baby* – babies).

this, that, these, those

- We use *this* and *that* to talk about one object.

  Is this your bag?
- We use *these* and *those* to talk about more than one object.

  Those actors are Italian.
- We use *this* and *these* to talk about things that are near.

  These are my shoes.
- We use *that* and *those* to talk about things that are not near.

  That's Khaled's house over there.

3.2

have/has

	Positive	Negative
I/you/we/they	**I have** a phone. **You have** a phone. **We have** a phone. **They have** a phone.	**I don't have** a son. **You don't have** a son. **We don't have** a son. **They don't have** a son.
he/she	**He has** a phone. **She has** a phone.	**He doesn't have** an umbrella.

	Question	Short answers
I/you/we/they	**Do I/you/we/they have** children?	**Yes, I/you/we/they do.** **No, I/you/we/they don't.**
he/she	**Does he/she have** a red bag?	**Yes, he/she does.** **No, he/she doesn't.**

- We use *have/has* to talk about family members and things that we own.

3.1

a/an and plural nouns

A Choose *a* or *an* or no article (–) to complete the sentences and questions.

1 My grandmother has ***a*** / ***an*** / (–) glasses.
2 ***A*** / ***An*** / – headphones are useful.
3 Aisha doesn't have ***a*** / ***an*** / – coat.
4 Is there ***a*** / ***an*** / – address on the letter?
5 This is ***a*** / ***an*** / – map of Turkey.
6 Take ***a*** / ***an*** / – umbrella with you!

B Complete the sentences and questions with the plural form of the words in parentheses.

1 Put three ___*tomatoes*___ (*tomato*) in the salad.
2 Our ______ (*family*) live on the same street.
3 When are your piano ______ (*lesson*)?
4 Which ______ (*country*) are on the map?
5 My team isn't playing well – we have five ______ (*loss*)!

this, that, these, those

C Complete the sentences and questions with *is* or *are*.

1 This phone ___*is*___ great!
2 ______ that a map of Greece?
3 These ______ my new shoes.
4 These exercises ______ easy!
5 What ______ that thing over there?
6 ______ these Olivia's headphones?

D Read the sentences and check (✓) the correct pictures.

1 This is my new hat.

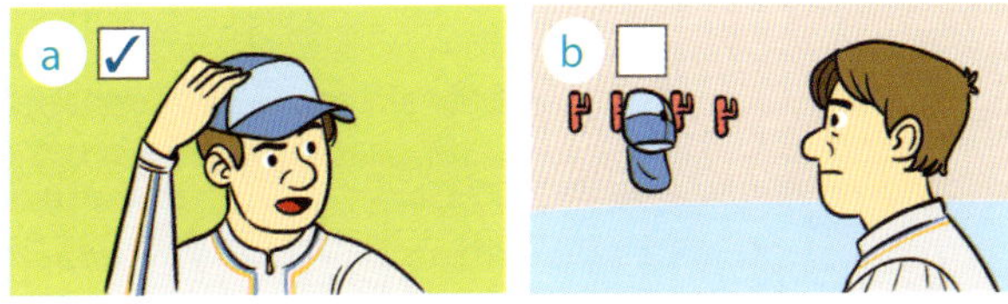

2 That is my book.

3 Those headphones are cool!

4 Are these your keys?

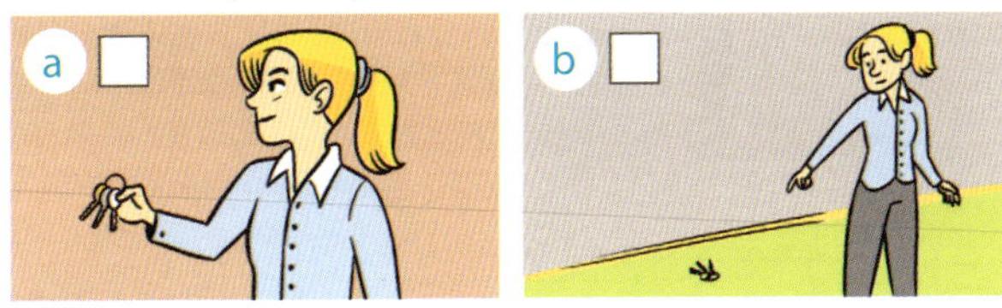

➤ Go back to page 19.

3.2

have/has

A Complete the sentences with the correct form of *have*.

1 Afua ___*doesn't have*___ a coat and she's cold! (-)
2 My friends and I ______ English classes on Sundays. (-)
3 My mother ______ a new phone. (+)
4 I ______ a brother. (+)
5 Akim ______ a blue school bag. (+)
6 My dad ______ glasses. (-)
7 She ______ a brother and a sister. (+)
8 We ______ a new car. (+)
9 They ______ grandchildren. (-)
10 Sarah ______ a coat. (-)

B Put the words in order to make questions. Then write short answers.

1 my phone / have / Do / you
A: *Do you have my phone* ______?
B: No, ___*I don't*___.

2 have / Carlo / a brother / Does
A: ______?
B: No, ______.

3 have / they / a red car / Do
A: ______?
B: Yes, ______.

4 two grandchildren / Mary and John / have / Do
A: ______?
B: Yes, ______.

5 the waiter / have / our food / Does
A: ______?
B: Yes, ______.

➤ Go back to page 21.

Grammar Hub

4.1

Simple present: *I, you, we, they*

	Positive	Negative
I	**I work** in an office.	**I do not work** in an office. **I don't work** in an office.
you	**You start** work at eight o'clock.	**You do not start** work at eight o'clock. **You don't start** work at eight o'clock.
we	**We watch** TV in the evening.	**We do not watch** TV in the evening. **We don't watch** TV in the evening.
they	**They play** soccer.	**They do not play** soccer. **They don't play** soccer.

- We use the simple present for things that are always true or actions that always happen.
  They live in a lighthouse.
  We play soccer on Saturdays.
- For *I/you/we/they*, the verb form is the same.
  I play.
  We play.
- We form the negative with the long form (*do not*) or the contraction (*don't*) before the verb. We usually use the contraction when we speak.
  I do not start work at nine o'clock. OR I don't start work at nine o'clock.

Be careful!

- Remember that *don't* is the negative of *do not*.
  I don't work here. NOT ~~I don't not work here.~~

4.2

Simple present questions: *I, you, we, they*

	Yes/No question	Positive short answer	Negative short answer
I	**Do I** live in a house?	**Yes, you do.**	**No, you don't.**
you	**Do you go** to the river?	**Yes, I/we do.**	**No, I/we don't.**
we	**Do we live** in houses?	**Yes, you do.**	**No, you don't.**
they	**Do they go** to the countryside?	**Yes, they do.**	**No, they don't.**

	Wh- questions
I/you/we/they	**What time do I start** work? **How do you relax**? **Where do we live**? **When do they go** to work?

- For *yes/no* questions, we put *do* at the beginning. We don't change the verb.
  Do you work here?
- For other questions we can use question words, e.g. *where, when, what time, who, how*, etc. We put *do* after the question word.
  Where do you live?
  When do we start work?

Be careful!

- For negative answers to *yes/no* questions, we normally use the contraction.
  No, I don't. NOT ~~No, I do not.~~

4.1

Simple present: *I, you, we, they*

A Choose the correct options.

1 I *don't* / *not* watch TV in the mornings.
2 They *do go* / *go* to bed at 11 pm.
3 After work, we go home and *to relax* / *relax*.
4 I *don't* / *not* get up early on Sundays.
5 I *am live* / *live* with two friends.
6 We *start* / *do start* work at seven in the morning.
7 You *go* / *to go* out on Saturdays.
8 They *play don't* / *don't play* games on their computers at work.

B Complete the text with the verbs in the box.

don't talk	finish	get up	go	live	relax	start	~~work~~

I [1] ______ in an office. My friends Anna and Frieda work there too. They're very nice. We [2] ______ work at 8 am, so I [3] ______ at 7 am. When we [4] ______ work – at about five o'clock, we [5] ______ out. Our other friends [6] ______ in the town, so we meet them after work. We [7] ______ and we [8] ______ about work!

C Reorder the words to make sentences.

1 don't / at six o'clock / I / get up ______.
2 TV / in the evenings / watch / I ______.
3 at seven o'clock / work / don't / you / start ______.
4 live / we / in the same house ______.
5 games / on my computer / play / I ______.
6 on Monday evenings / don't / we / go out ______.
7 they / here / don't / live ______.
8 I / at home / relax ______.

➤ Go back to page 27.

4.2

Simple present questions: *I, you, we, they*

A Match the questions (1–6) and the answers (a–f).

1 Do you live in Texas? ___
2 When do we start work? ___
3 Where do they live? ___
4 Do they work in August? ___
5 How do you relax? ___
6 Who do you work with? ___

a In Madrid.
b I watch TV.
c Yes, I do.
d No, they don't.
e Erica.
f At six o'clock.

B Complete the sentences with the words in the box.

do (x2)	don't	how	when	where

1 **A:** Do you both live in Warsaw?
B: Yes, we ______.

2 **A:** ______ do you live?
B: In Switzerland.

3 **A:** Do those people work with you?
B: No, they ______.

4 **A:** ______ do you get to work?
B: By car.

5 **A:** ______ do you watch TV?
B: In the evening.

6 **A:** Do you go to bed late?
B: Yes, I ______. I go to bed at about one o'clock in the morning.

C Use the prompts to write questions.

1 you / live / in a tent ______?
2 where / you / work ______?
3 you / play / games ______?
4 when / you / talk / to your family ______?
5 what time / you / start work ______?
6 your friends / live here ______?
7 how / we / play this game ______?
8 you / go / to the countryside ______?

➤ Go back to page 29.

Grammar Hub

5.1

Simple present: *he, she, it*

	Positive	Negative
he/she/it	**He cooks** dinner every day. **She washes** the dishes after dinner.	**He doesn't go running** in the morning. **She doesn't do** the laundry every day.

	Yes/No question	Short answer
he/she/it	**Does Henry take** a bath in the evening? **Does it clean** the floor?	**Yes, he does. / No, he doesn't.** **Yes, it does. / No, it doesn't.**

- In positive sentences with *he, she* or *it*, we use the main verb plus *-s* or *-es*.

  He cooks dinner for his family.
  She does housework in the afternoon.
- In negative sentences with *he, she* or *it*, we use *doesn't* plus the main verb without *-s*.

  Brad doesn't clean the bathroom.
  She doesn't watch TV all the time.
- In *yes/no* questions with *he, she* or *it*, we use *does* followed by the subject and the main verb without *-s*.

  Does your mom do your laundry for you?
- In *wh-* questions with *he, she* or *it*, we use a subject and *does* plus the main verb without *-s*.

  When does Martin make his bed?
- We use *does* in short answers to *yes/no* questions. We do not repeat the main verb.

  Does Tom clean the kitchen? Yes, he does. NOT ~~*Yes, he does clean.*~~

Be careful!

- Some verbs take *-es* for the ending in *he/she/it* simple present. Some examples are *do* and *go* and verbs that end in *-sh* or *-ch*.

  He does the laundry at night. NOT ~~*He dos the laundry at night.*~~
  She washes dishes with her sister. NOT ~~*She washs dishes with her sister.*~~

5.2

Adverbs of frequency

Adverb	Examples with *be*	Examples with other verbs
always	I'm **always** hungry!	I **always** drink coffee with breakfast.
usually	He's **usually** thirsty after running.	He **usually** eats dinner at 7 pm.
frequently	They're **frequently** late for dinner.	They **frequently** eat lunch in their office.
sometimes	You're **sometimes** tired and hungry.	You **sometimes** have coffee after lunch.
seldom	We are **seldom** free for coffee.	You **seldom** have dessert.
never	I'm **never** late for dinner.	I **never** drink orange juice.

(100% ↓ 0%)

- We put adverbs of frequency after the verb *be*.

  He's usually very hungry before lunch.
  They're sometimes busy on weekends.
- We put adverbs of frequency before other verbs.

  I usually have a large salad for supper.
  She frequently drinks water at lunchtime.
- We can also put the adverbs *usually* and *sometimes* at the beginning of the sentence.

  Usually, I have fruit for my breakfast.
  Sometimes, I have coffee.

Be careful!

- We don't put the adverbs *always, seldom* or *never* at the beginning of a sentence.

  She always has rice. NOT ~~*Always, she has rice.*~~

Be careful!

- We do not use *never* with *don't* or *doesn't*.

  I never eat late at night. NOT ~~*I don't never eat late at night.*~~

5.1

Simple present: *he, she, it*

A Choose the correct options.

1 He ___ for a walk every weekend.
a go (b) goes

2 She ___ meals for her children.
a cook b cooks

3 George doesn't ___ in the backyard at night.
a sit b sits

4 What gym does Monica ___ to?
a goes b go

5 Does Taylor ___ chess every day?
a plays b play

6 Does he go running late at night? Yes, he ___.
a does b runs

7 Kelly ___ TV on Saturday mornings.
a watchs b watches

8 What time does Jenny ___ a bath?
a take b takes

B Check (✓) the correct sentences and put an (✗) for the incorrect sentences.

1 David sits in the backyard in the evening. ✓
2 Mike go running every Sunday. ___
3 Jill cooks meals for her family. ___
4 Paula doesn't plays chess every day. ___
5 Does Josh goes to the gym? ___
6 **A:** Does Henry go shopping?
B: Yes, he does. ___
7 **A:** Does Amy take a bath every day?
B: No, she doesn't do! ___
8 Where Erika goes for a walk? ___

C Complete the sentences with the correct form of the words in parentheses.

1 Michelle ___*sits*___ (*sit*) in the backyard in the summer.
2 My dad ______ (*take*) a bath every night.
3 She ______ (*go*) for a walk every weekend.
4 When ______ (*he / do*) the laundry?
5 **A:** Does your grandmother go running?
B: No, she ______ (*do not*).
6 Lily ______ (*not go*) to the gym.
7 **A:** Does your brother play chess?
B: Yes, he ______ (*do*).

➤ Go back to page 35.

5.2

Adverbs of frequency

A Choose the correct adverbs of frequency.

1 I ___ have coffee in the morning, but not every day.
a always (b) frequently

2 She ___ has salad for lunch. She has it three or four times a week.
a never b frequently

3 He ___ eats eggs for breakfast. He doesn't like them!
a sometimes b never

4 They ___ have dinner at home, five or six days a week.
a never b usually

5 She's ___ early for class, two or three times a month.
a sometimes b always

6 We ___ cook chicken and rice. My wife and I don't like it.
a never b usually

7 John is ___ busy on Fridays. He has a lot of work on that day.
a always b never

8 You ___ eat snacks, almost every day of the week!
a sometimes b frequently

B Choose the correct options to complete the sentences.

1 Mike (*usually has*) / *has usually* juice with his cereal.
2 She *cooks frequently* / *frequently cooks* dinner for the family.
3 They *frequently are* / *are frequently* late for class.
4 We *drink never* / *never drink* milk at breakfast.
5 I *am sometimes* / *sometimes am* hungry for breakfast.
6 He *seldom eats* / *eats seldom* vegetables.
7 You *always aren't* / *aren't always* busy for lunch.
8 Helena doesn't *never* / *usually* eat bananas.

C Put the words in the correct order to make sentences.

1 drink / usually / for / I / breakfast / tea
I usually drink tea for breakfast.
2 home / cooks / she / dinner / at / frequently
______.
3 in / hungry / morning / the / he / is / always
______.
4 breakfast / eat / we / never
______.
5 don't / pizza / usually / they / have
______.
6 for / are / never / we / work / late
______.

➤ Go back to page 37.

Grammar Hub

6.1

there is / there are

	Singular	Plural
Positive	**There is** a bus stop. **There's** a bus stop.	**There are** a lot of boats.
Negative	**There isn't** an airport.	**There aren't** any buses.

- We use *there is/isn't* or *there are/aren't* to say that something exists (or doesn't exist). We can use *there is / there are* to describe different places or things in a house, town, etc.

  There are a lot of flowers in the yard.
  There's a bookstore in the center of town.
- We use *there is* with a singular noun and *there are* with a plural noun.

  There's a bank in the city center.
  There are bus stops on this street.
- We use *some* and *a lot of* with plural nouns in positive sentences.

  There are some nice cafés in my neighborhood.
  There are a lot of hotels in this city.
- We use *any* and *a lot of* with plural nouns in negative sentences.

  There aren't any museums in my town.
  There aren't a lot of tourists here.

	some / a lot of / any
Positive	There are **some** big buildings. There are **a lot of** museums.
Negative	There aren't **any** islands. There aren't **a lot of** stores.

Be careful!

- In sentences with more than one noun, the verb agrees with the first noun.

  There's a hotel and a grocery store.
  There are ten stores and a large hotel.
  There's a park and two swimming pools.

6.2

***is there / are there* question forms**

	Question	Positive short answer	Negative short answer
Singular	**Is there** a dresser?	**Yes, there is.**	**No, there isn't.**
Plural	**Are there** cushions?	**Yes, there are.**	**No, there aren't.**

	Question
a lot of	Are there **a lot of** books?
any	Are there **any** chairs?

- We use *Is there …?* or *Are there …?* to ask about different places and objects.

  Is there a library in town?
  Are there cushions on the couch?
- We use *Is there …?* with a singular noun and *Are there …?* with a plural noun.

  Is there a bathtub in the bathroom?
  Are there pictures on the wall?
- We can use *a lot of* and *any* in questions about plural nouns.

  Are there a lot of books on the bookshelf?
  Are there any cups in the kitchen?

Be careful!

- We use *there is* not *there's* in a positive short answer.

  Yes, there is. NOT ~~*Yes, there's.*~~

6.1

There is / There are

A Choose the correct options to complete the sentences.

1 There aren't *some* / *any* cars in Venice.
2 There are *a lot of* / *any* water taxis.
3 There *'s* / *are* 350 boats (called 'gondolas') in Venice.
4 There are about 400 boatmen but there *'s* / *are* only one woman!
5 There are *a* / *some* narrow streets in Venice. One street is only 53 centimeters wide!
6 There are *some* / *any* very old buildings in Venice – the Palazzo Grimani Museum is more than 500 years old!

B Complete the description with *there is/there isn't* or *there are/aren't*.

I live in a small town and [1] ___there aren't___ a lot of restaurants. [2] ______ one small café where you can get tea and coffee or juice. [3] ______ a lot of things to do in my town – it's very boring really – but [4] ______ a nice park. I usually play soccer there with my friends on Saturdays. It's a very small place, so [5] ______ any art galleries and [6] ______ a museum. You have to go to the city to find those, but [7] ______ two small stores. [8] ______ a train station and that's very important for me and my friends because we get the train into the city. In the city, [9] ______ a big shopping mall and we go there to buy clothes.

C Complete the sentences with the correct form of the noun in parentheses. Add *a* or *an* if necessary.

1 There are a lot of ___flowers___ (*flower*) in our yard.
2 There's a TV and ___a computer___ (*computer*).
3 There aren't any ______ (*book*) on the bookshelf.
4 There are ten ______ (*chair*) and a big table.
5 There's ______ (*fridge*) in the kitchen.
6 There isn't ______ (*apple tree*) in the backyard.
7 There aren't a lot of ______ (*plant*) on the balcony.
8 There are some ______ (*cushion*) on the floor.

➤ Go back to page 43.

6.2

***Is there / Are there* question forms**

A Complete the questions with *Is* or *Are*.

1 ___Is___ there a bookcase in your bedroom?
2 ______ there a big window?
3 ______ there two beds in your bedroom?
4 ______ there a lot of cushions on your couch?
5 ______ there any photos on the walls?
6 ______ there a TV in your bedroom?
7 ______ there a desk by the window?
8 ______ there a lot of things under your bed?

B Answer the questions in Exercise A.

1 Yes, there ___is___.
2 No, there ______.
3 Yes, there ______.
4 No, there ______.
5 Yes, there ______.
6 No, there ______.
7 Yes, there ______.
8 No, there ______.

C Use the prompts to create questions using *Is there* and *Are there*.

1 a lot of / cabinets / kitchen
______?
2 a lamp / desk
______?
3 any / books / bookshelf
______?
4 clock / wall
______?
5 cups / coffee table
______?
6 any / mirrors / bathroom
______?
7 blue cushions / couch
______?
8 rug / bedroom floor
______?

➤ Go back to page 45.

Grammar Hub

7.1

can / can't

	Positive	Negative
I/you/he/she/it/we/they	**I can** swim. **They can** fly.	**I can't** swim. **They can't** fly.

- We use *can/can't* when we want to talk about someone's ability or skills.

  I can run.
  I can't drive a car.
- The form of *can/can't* never changes.

  He can swim. NOT ~~He cans swim.~~
  She can't climb. NOT ~~She cans not climb.~~

	Question	Positive short answer	Negative short answer
I/you/he/she/it/we/they	**Can you** climb? **Can they** live underwater?	**Yes, I/we can.** **Yes, they can.**	**No, I/we can't.** **No, they can't.**

- We also ask *wh-* questions with *can*.

  What can you do?
  Which animals can fly?

Be careful!

- *Can* is followed by a verb without *to*.

  I can swim. NOT ~~I can to swim.~~

7.2

Possessive *'s*

Singular noun	This is **John's** sister.
Singular noun ending with -s	Is that **Chris's** brother? Is that **Chris'** brother?
Plural noun	These are the **girls'** friends.

- We use a possessive *'s* to show that something belongs to someone.

  This is Mark's bag. = This bag belongs to Mark.
- With a singular noun, we add *'s* to show something belongs to that person.

  This is the boy's dad.
- With a singular noun that ends in *-s*, we can add *'s* or *'* after the *-s*.

  This is James's sister.
  This is James' sister.
- For plural nouns that end in *-s*, we add the *'* after the *-s*.

  My cousins' house. (= I have more than one cousin and they share the same house.)
  What are your parents' names? (= You have more than one parent.)

Be careful!

- We also use *'s* as a contraction of *is* or *has*.

  *His name's Bill. (= his name **is**)*
  *He's been out with his brother. (= he **has**)*

7.1

can / can't

A Choose the correct options.

1 I can *walk* / *to walk* all day.
2 He *can't* / *not* speak English.
3 *Can you* / *You can* play chess?
4 I can swim but my brother *isn't* / *can't*.
5 *They can* / *Can they* climb with a rope?
6 **A:** Can you swim?
B: Yes I *can* / *swim*.
7 What things *can you* / *you can* do?
8 Dogs can swim but they *not* / *can't* fly.

B Write *can* or *can't* to complete the sentences.

1 We ______ climb this mountain – it's not that big!
2 Fish ______ fly.
3 My brother ______ speak French – he's terrible at languages.
4 Sam's manager ______ play the guitar. She's very talented.
5 She can drive a car but she ______ ride a motorcycle.

C Complete the short answers.

1 Can you swim? Yes, ______I can______.
2 Can you play guitar? No, ______.
3 Can they swim? Yes, ______.
4 Can John speak French? Yes, ______.
5 Can she speak Spanish? No, ______.
6 Can fish fly? No, ______.

D PRACTICE There is one mistake in each sentence. Correct the sentences.

1 I can to climb without ropes.
I can climb without ropes.
2 We not can jump very high.
______
3 It can flies for hundreds of kilometers.
______
4 He cans swim underwater for a long time.
______
5 Do you can dive ten meters down?
______
6 No, I don't can!
______
7 They can do play musical instruments.
______
8 We can to run very far.
______
9 She can speaks English.
______
10 Yes, I do can.
______

➤ Go back to page 50.

7.2

Possessive *'s*

A There is one mistake in each sentence. Find and correct the mistakes.

1 This is my ~~friend~~ *friend's* sister, Mary.
2 Sebastian is Fiona brother.
3 John's brothers names are Philip and Frederick.
4 My sisters' name is Sandra.
5 I like Davids' house.
6 Do you know Angus manager?
7 These are my parent's, Jill and Greg.
8 Where is Harry's parents house?

B Rewrite the phrases using *'s* or *'*.

1 the uncle of my friend = ______*my friend's uncle*______
2 the office of Costas = ______
3 the names of my parents = ______
4 the favorite restaurant of Keith = ______
5 the daughter of my manager = ______
6 the company of his cousins = ______
7 the school of their sons = ______
8 the desk of Peter = ______

C Read the text and write *'s* or *'* in the correct places. There are six changes, including the example.

I have a busy week this week. On Monday, there's an all-day meeting in my manager*'s* office, starting at 9 am. Then, I have to go to my son school (I have a son and a daughter) to talk to his teachers. On Tuesday, I go to Tampa for three days. We usually go in my colleague car. I always stay at a friend house in Tampa. My parents live near there, so I usually see them. My parents house is very small, so I can't stay there. Then, on Friday, we have a meeting at our company Orlando office. Finally, my vacation starts on Saturday!

➤ Go back to page 53.

Grammar Hub

8.1

Present progressive

	Positive	Negative
I	**I am talking** to my neighbor. **I'm talking** to my neighbor.	**I am not wearing** a green coat. **I'm not wearing** a green coat.
you/we/they	**We are sitting** in a café. **We're sitting** in a café.	**They are not leaving** the park. **They aren't leaving** the park. **They're not leaving** the park.
he/she/it	**It is raining** right now. **It's raining** right now.	**She is not working** at her desk. **She isn't working** at her desk. **She's not working** at her desk.

	Question	Positive short answer	Negative short answer
I	**Am I sitting** in your chair?	**Yes, you are.**	**No, you aren't. / No, you're not.**
you/we/they	**Are you drinking** coffee?	**Yes, I am.** **Yes, we are.**	**No, I'm not.** **No, we aren't. / No, we're not.**
he/she/it	**Is he taking** a selfie?	**Yes, he is.**	**No, he isn't. / No, he's not.**

- We use the present progressive to talk about things that happen now.
  I'm going to the library right now.
- We make the present progressive with the subject + *am/is/are* + verb + *-ing*.
  We're walking down the street.
  She's standing up now.
- In questions, the subject goes after *am/is/are*.
  Are you meeting your friends?
- In positive short answers, we use the subject + *am/is/are*.
  Is Malcolm watching TV right now? Yes, he is.
- In negative short answers with *you/he/she/it/we/they*, there's a choice of negative.
  Is Greg watching TV right now? No, he isn't. OR No, he's not.

Be careful!

- We cannot use the present progressive to talk about things we do every day, only for things we're doing right now.
  I'm drinking tea with my breakfast today. NOT ~~I'm drinking tea with my breakfast every day.~~
- We add *-ing* to the verb to make the present progressive. Some verbs have special spelling rules. For verbs that end in a consonant + *-e*, such as *have*, *come* and *make*, we cut the *-e* and add *-ing*.
  He's coming from the library. NOT ~~He's comeing from the library.~~
- For most verbs that end in consonant + vowel + consonant, such as *sit*, *stop* and *put*, we double the consonant and add *-ing*.
  They're stopping at the bank. NOT ~~They're stoping at the bank.~~

8.2

Adjective order

	Size	Age	Color
Adjectives	**big** **short** **long**	**new** **old**	**red** **yellow** **green** **blue** **gray** **white**
Example sentences	It's a **big red** coat. He's wearing **old green** shorts. We're wearing our **new blue** shoes.		

- We can put more than one adjective before a noun.
  I'm wearing a new red shirt.
  He has a big gray hat.
- The color adjective usually goes after the adjective for size or age.
  It's an old yellow dress. NOT ~~It's a yellow old dress.~~

Be careful!

- Remember to use the right article before the adjective. We use *an* in front of adjectives that start with a vowel.
  She's wearing an old blue dress. NOT ~~She's wearing a old blue dress.~~

8.1

Present progressive

A Choose the correct options.

1 I'm *walking* / *walk* down the street.
2 You *are* / *is* sitting on my coat.
3 We're not *watch* / *watching* the movie now.
4 *Is she* / *She is* meeting her friend now?
5 He's *stand* / *standing* up right now.
6 They're *not looking* / *looking not* at clothes.
7 Are you *have* / *having* lunch now?
8 We're *going* / *go* to the park.

B Choose the correct answers to the questions.

1 Are you texting Darren?
a No, you're not. (b) No, I'm not.
2 Is your sister having lunch?
a Yes, she is. b Yes, she has.
3 Are they going to the bank?
a No, they're not going. b No, they're not.
4 Am I wearing your T-shirt?
a Yes, it is. b Yes, you are.
5 Is he lying down right now?
a Yes, he's lying. b Yes, he is.
6 Is Harry sleeping?
a No, he's not. b No, he not sleeping.
7 Are they talking to someone?
a No, they're not talking. b No, they aren't.
8 Are you watching the soccer game?
a Yes, I am. b Yes, I'm.

C Complete the sentences with the present progressive form of the verbs in parentheses.

1 He ___is walking___ (*walk*) to the park.
2 She ______ (*eat*) dinner now.
3 They ______ (*sit*) on a bench.
4 I ______ (*have*) a salad.
5 ______ (*you / wear*) your new coat?
6 Look! The car ______. (*not stop*)
7 ______ (*she / make*) dinner?
8 I ______ (*put*) money in the bank.

➤ Go back to page 58.

8.2

Adjective order

A Choose the correct options.

1 It's a ___ coat.
(a) new red b red new
2 She has ___ shoes.
a green old b old green
3 He's wearing a ___ hat.
a big blue b blue big
4 Do you have a ___ dress?
a new green b green new
5 I like your ___ skirt.
a yellow long b long yellow
6 They don't have ___ sneakers.
a white new b new white
7 It's a(n) ___ sweatshirt.
a gray old b old gray
8 Michelle is wearing a ___ coat.
a short white b white short

B Check (✓) the correct sentences and put an (✗) for the incorrect sentences.

1 She's wearing red long socks. ✗
2 He likes old yellow hats. ___
3 It's a gray big dress. ___
4 Those aren't new brown shoes. ___
5 They're not wearing long green skirts. ___
6 We have blue old T-shirts. ___
7 I want a big white sweatshirt. ___
8 Do you have green new shoes? ___

C Put the words in the correct order to make sentences and questions.

1 socks / brown / they're / old
___They're old brown socks___.
2 has / red / coat / she / a / big
______.
3 wearing / green / they're / old / T-shirts
______.
4 you / hat / new / a / have / brown / do
______?
5 coat / like / I / blue / your / long
______.
6 a / sweatshirt / yellow / that's / big
______.

➤ Go back to page 61.

Grammar Hub

9.1

Simple past: *was/were*

	Positive	Negative
I/he/she/it	**It was** interesting.	**She was not** young. **She wasn't** young.
you/we/they	**You were** amazing.	**We were not** there. **We weren't** there.

	Question	Positive short answer	Negative short answer
I/he/she/it	**Was he** popular?	**Yes, he was.**	**No, he wasn't.**
you/we/they	**Were they** at home?	**Yes, they were.**	**No, they weren't.**

- The simple past forms of the verb *be* are *was, were, wasn't* and *weren't*.

  Marie Tussaud was an artist from France.

  My grandparents weren't famous.
- We use *was(n't)/were(n't)* to talk about people and things in the past.

  Nelson Mandela was the first black president of South Africa.
- For *yes/no* questions, we put *was* or *were* at the beginning of the question, followed by the subject.

  Was he a popular writer?
- For *wh-* questions, we put *what, where, why*, etc at the beginning of the question, followed by *was/were* + the subject.

  Who was that man?

  Where was it?

  Why were you late?

9.2

Simple past: regular verbs

	Positive	Negative
I/you/he/she/it/we/they	**She lived** in Mexico. **We learned** a song.	**I did not play** tennis. **I didn't play** tennis.

- We use the simple past tense to talk about actions in the past.

  Alexander Fleming discovered penicillin in 1928.
- We form the simple past tense of regular verbs by adding *-ed* to the main verb. If the verb ends in *-e*, just add *-d*. If the verb ends in *-y*, change the *-y* to an *-i* and add *-ed*.

  start → *started*

  live → *lived*

  study → *studied*
- To form the negative, we put *did not* (*didn't*) before the main verb.

  She didn't study math.
- To talk about a period of time in the past, we can use *for* + minutes, months, years, etc.

  He lived in Spain for three years.

Be careful!

- Use *didn't* for the negative, but don't add *-d* or *-ed* to the main verb. The main verb stays the same.

  She didn't live there. NOT ~~*She didn't lived there.*~~

9.1

Simple past: *was/were*

A Complete the conversation with *was*, *wasn't*, *were* or *weren't*.

A: Where [1] ___were___ you yesterday?

B: I [2] ______ in London.

A: Why [3] ______ you in London?

B: We [4] ______ at Madame Tussauds on a day trip.

A: [5] ______ it fun?

B: Yes, it [6] ______ amazing. There were statues of writers, actors and politicians. They [7] ______ all so real!

A: [8] ______ you there all day?

B: No, we [9] ______. We [10] ______ there for about three hours.

B Put the words in the correct order to make questions.

1 Charles Dickens / was / who ___Who was Charles Dickens___?
2 when / he / was / born ______?
3 he / from London / was ______?
4 from / where / he / was ______?
5 rich / were / his parents ______?
6 his best book / what / was ______?

C Match the questions (1–6) in Exercise B and the answers (a–f).

___ **a** No, he wasn't.
___ **b** It was *Oliver Twist*, in my opinion.
___ **c** He was a famous writer.
___ **d** No, they weren't.
___ **e** He was born in 1812.
___ **f** He was from Portsmouth.

➤ Go back to page 67.

9.2

Simple past: regular verbs

A Complete the sentences with the simple past form of the verbs in parentheses.

1 Picasso ___changed___ (*change*) the way we look at art.
2 We ______ (*try*) to find information about Frida Kahlo.
3 William Shakespeare ______ (*live*) in a town called Stratford-upon-Avon.
4 Kim ______ (*decide*) to write about Ada Lovelace for her project.
5 The women ______ (*plant*) trees in the park.
6 I ______ (*start*) to read a book about famous women scientists.
7 Our history class ______ (*study*) the Anasazi people of North America last year.
8 Shelly ______ (*remember*) to bring back my book about Wangari Maathai.

B Make the sentences negative.

1 Ada Lovelace studied art.
Ada Lovelace ___didn't study art___.
2 The female characters talked a lot in the book.
The female characters ______ in the book.
3 Elena Favilli and Francesca Cavallo created a book about famous men.
Elena Favilli and Francesca Cavallo ______.
4 Maria Sibylla Merian collected clothes.
Maria Sibylla Merian ______.
5 Wangari Maathai planted flowers.
Wangari Maathai ______.

C Complete the sentences with the past form of the verbs in parentheses.

1 I ______ (*not want*) to be a dancer when I was a child.
2 We ______ (*study*) French when we were at school.
3 My wife ______ (*design*) the house we live in.
4 He ______ (*start*) a new yoga class last week.
5 She ______ (*not use*) her phone yesterday.
6 They ______ (*not receive*) the letter last Monday.

➤ Go back to page 69.

Grammar Hub

10.1

Simple past: irregular verbs

Verb	Positive	Negative
build	**I built** a house.	**I didn't build** a house.
buy	**You bought** a good car.	**You didn't buy** a good car.
choose	**He chose** 100 objects.	**He didn't choose** 100 objects.
find	**She found** it yesterday.	**She didn't find** it yesterday.
give	**We gave** it to the teacher.	**We didn't give** it to the teacher.
go	**They went** from town to town.	**They didn't go** from town to town.
have	**I had** coffee this morning.	**I didn't have** coffee this morning.
make	**They made** tools.	**They didn't make** tools.
sell	**We sold** the house.	**We didn't sell** the house.
wear	**She wore** her new T-shirt yesterday.	**She didn't wear** her new T-shirt yesterday.

- Irregular verbs do not take *-ed* in the simple past. You have to learn each verb separately.
  They found an axe. NOT ~~*They finded an axe.*~~
  They went to the museum. NOT ~~*They goed to the museum.*~~
- In the negative, we use *didn't* + base form.
  I didn't have coffee yesterday. NOT ~~*I didn't had coffee yesterday.*~~
- In the negative, we usually use the contraction *didn't* but we can also use the long form *did not*.
  They didn't know the answer. OR *They did not know the answer.*

Be careful!

- Irregular verbs do not change form in the simple past.
  simple present: I make… / He makes… BUT simple past: I made… / He made…

10.2

Simple past: questions

Question	Positive short answer	Negative short answer
Did I tell you about the meeting?	**Yes, you did.**	**No, you didn't.**
Did you see the manager?	**Yes, I/we did.**	**No, I/we didn't.**
Did he win a prize?	**Yes, he did.**	**No, he didn't.**
Did she finish her work?	**Yes, she did.**	**No, she didn't.**
Did it rain yesterday?	**Yes, it did.**	**No, it didn't.**
Did we take a lot of photos?	**Yes, you/we did.**	**No, you/we didn't.**
Did they find the money?	**Yes, they did.**	**No, they didn't.**

- For *yes/no* questions, we put *did* at the beginning, followed by the subject + base form. We don't change the verb.
  Did you see that?

	Wh- questions
I/you/he/she/it/we/they	**What time did she get up**?
	How did you get to work today?
	Where did they study?
	When did he leave Jamaica?
	Why did you do that?
	Who did you talk to yesterday?

- For *wh-* questions, we put *what*, *where*, *why*, etc at the beginning of the question, followed by *did* + subject + base form.
  Where did she go?
  Who did they work with?
  What did she say?

Be careful!

- For negative answers to *yes/no* questions, we normally use the contraction.
  No, I didn't. NOT ~~*No, I did not.*~~

10.1

Simple past: irregular verbs

A Write the simple past form of the verbs.

1 have ___had___
2 make ______
3 go ______
4 build ______
5 sell ______
6 buy ______
7 give ______
8 wear ______

B Complete the sentences using the simple past form of the verbs in parentheses.

1 I ___wore___ (*wear*) a blue shirt yesterday.
2 My dad ______ (*build*) our house.
3 We ______ (*have*) coffee for breakfast.
4 Our parents ______ (*give*) us money.
5 He ______ (*buy*) a new phone.
6 They ______ (*choose*) a present for Alan.
7 My grandmother ______ (*sell*) flowers.
8 You ______ (*find*) us.

C Rewrite the sentences in Exercise B in the negative.

1 ___I didn't wear a blue shirt yesterday___.
2 ______.
3 ______.
4 ______.
5 ______.
6 ______.
7 ______.
8 ______.

D Complete the sentences with the correct simple past form of the verbs in parentheses.

A hundred years ago, life in America was very different. They [1] ______ (*not have*) computers or cell phones. People [2] ______ (*not send*) emails. They [3] ______ (*write*) letters and [4] ______ (*send*) postcards. They [5] ______ (*not buy*) things online. They [6] ______ (*go*) to stores and markets. Stores [7] ______ (*not sell*) a lot of clothes. People [8] ______ (*make*) clothes at home. Parents [9] ______ (*give*) their children homemade toys. But even without the internet, children [10] ______ (*find*) a lot of ways to have fun by singing and playing games at home.

➤ Go back to page 74.

10.2

Simple past questions

A Match the questions (1–6) and the answers (a–f).

1 Did they watch TV last night? ___d___
2 What time did you get up? ___
3 Where did you go on vacation? ___
4 Did you go to work yesterday? ___
5 How did you get to work? ___
6 Did it start on time? ___

a To Florida.
b No, it didn't.
c Yes, I did.
d No, they didn't.
e I went by bus.
f At nine o'clock.

B Complete the sentences with the words in the box.

did ~~didn't~~ we what where why

1 **A:** Did you sell him your car?
B: No, I ___didn't___.
2 **A:** ______ did you buy those clothes?
B: In town.
3 **A:** How ______ you get here?
B: By car.
4 **A:** Did you find us OK?
B: Yes, ______ did.
5 **A:** ______ did you buy that phone?
B: Because I liked it.
6 **A:** ______ time did the movie start?
B: At eight o'clock.

C Write questions in the simple past.

1 you / see / that
___Did you see that___?
2 when / you / go / to Miami
______?
3 you / build / your house
______?
4 where / you / buy / that hat
______?
5 she / wear / her new dress
______?
6 why / you / choose / that color
______?
7 they / find / the money
______?
8 what time / we / start
______?

➤ Go back to page 77.

Grammar Hub

11.1

like/love/hate/enjoy* + verb + *-ing

	Positive	Negative	Question
I/you/we/they	**I enjoy going** to the theater. **They love going** to restaurants.	**We don't enjoy staying** at home on weekends.	**Do they like spending** time with friends?
he/she/it	**He likes watching** TV. **Joanna loves playing** soccer.	**She doesn't like listening** to loud music.	**Does Frank enjoy watching** videos on his laptop?

- In positive phrases, we use *like/love/hate/enjoy* + verb + *-ing*.

  I like going to concerts.

  We love getting takeout food.
- In negative phrases, we use *don't/doesn't* + *like/love/hate/enjoy* + verb + *-ing*.

  I don't enjoy watching movies on my laptop.

  He doesn't like going to soccer games.
- In questions, we use *do/does* + subject + *like/love/hate/enjoy* + verb + *-ing*.

  Do you enjoy listening to music?

  Does Harriet like watching videos online?

Be careful!

- Make sure you put only the activity verb in the *-ing* form and not *like/love/hate/enjoy*.

  I like spending time with my friends. NOT ~~I'm liking spending time with my friends.~~

11.2

Object pronouns

Subject pronoun	Object pronoun
I like soccer.	Sam plays soccer with **me**.
You know many people.	Many people know **you**.
He enjoys movies.	Mike watches movies with **him**.
She doesn't like TV.	Audrie doesn't watch TV with **her**.
We are musicians.	People like listening to **us**.
Do **they** play tennis?	Do Raphael and Sue play with **them**?

- We can use object pronouns to refer to object nouns.

  *The children like **Raphael**. = The children like **him**.*

  *Erin doesn't like **the videos**. = Erin doesn't like **them**.*

  *Does Helen know **Paulina**? = Does Helen know **her**?*
- Subject pronouns are *I, you, he, she, it, we* and *they*. Object pronouns are *me, you, him, her, it, us* and *them*.

  I like my teachers. My teachers like me. I like them.

  Tennis is a sport. It is fun, but Gus and Vicky don't like it.

  Leslie sings in a band. She's a good singer, and I love her.
- Object pronouns can follow *with* and *to*.

  Josh plays soccer with him.

  Do you like listening to them?

Be careful!

- Use *it* for singular object nouns, and *them* for plural object nouns.

  Mary likes that show. She watches it online. NOT ~~She watches them online.~~

  Tom hates soccer games. He doesn't watch them. NOT ~~He doesn't watch it.~~

11.1

like/love/hate/enjoy + verb + _-ing_

A Choose the correct options to complete the sentences.

1 We *enjoy* / *enjoys* going to the movie theater.
2 He *likes* / *like* watching TV shows on his laptop.
3 They *love* / *loves* spending time with family.
4 *Do* / *Does* Jenny hate going to concerts?
5 I *don't* / *doesn't* like playing tennis.
6 You *like* / *likes* seeing friends on weekends.
7 *Does* / *Do* they enjoy playing soccer?
8 He *don't* / *doesn't* like listening to music.

B Complete the sentences with the correct form of the verbs in parentheses.

1 I don't like ___doing___ (*do*) homework on weekends.
2 She loves ________ (*go*) out in her free time.
3 Do you hate ________ (*stay*) in the house all day?
4 Henry doesn't like ________ (*talk*) to his friends online.
5 They love ________ (*chat*) with people from all over the world.
6 We don't enjoy ________ (*make*) dinner at home.
7 Does Jim like ________ (*get*) takeout food?
8 I enjoy ________ (*see*) my friends on the weekend.

C Use the words in parentheses to complete the text.

My friend Lukas [1] ________ (*hate / stay*) in. He's a writer and he works at home, so in the evening he [2] ________ (*not like / watch*) TV. He wants to go out. Every evening! He [3] ________ (*enjoy / go*) to a café or a restaurant, and he [4] ________ (*love / go*) to the movie theater and the theater. I frequently go out with him, but I [5] ________ (*not like / go*) out every night – it's too expensive!

➤ Go back to page 83.

11.2

Object pronouns

A Choose the correct options to complete the sentences.

1 I usually play soccer with my brother. He likes playing with ___.
   (a) me   b I
2 Danielle watches movies with her sister. She usually goes to the movie theater with ___.
   a she   b her
3 We like pop music, but we don't listen to ___ all the time.
   a them   b it
4 There are a lot of games at our stadium, but I don't frequently see ___.
   a them   b it
5 My favorite actor is Ryan Gosling. I like ___ and his movies a lot!
   a him   b he
6 Simon and I play tennis with my neighbor, Dina. She really enjoys playing with ___.
   a her   b us

B Rewrite the words in bold using object pronouns.

1 Cat videos are funny. Jill enjoys watching **cat videos**. ___them___
2 Lionel Messi is a great player. Mike and I love **Lionel Messi**! ________
3 Rihanna is a famous singer. Michelle likes listening to **Rihanna**. ________
4 Jake loves playing soccer. I don't like **soccer**. ________
5 Jan and I watch TV with my little brother. He likes spending time with **me and Jan**. ________

C Choose the correct options to complete the conversation.

Thomas: Who's a famous person in your home country, Anika?
Anika: Aishwarya Rai is a famous actress in India. Do you know [1]*it* / *her*?
Thomas: Yes, I think so. She's famous in the US, too. Do you enjoy watching her movies?
Anika: Yes, I do. I frequently watch [2]*her* / *them*. Who's your favorite actress or actor?
Thomas: I really like Benedict Cumberbatch. He's great in the TV show *Sherlock*. I enjoy seeing [3]*him* / *he* as Sherlock Holmes.
Anika: Yes, he's very good. *Sherlock* is a good show, but I don't watch [4]*it* / *him* regularly.
Thomas: And what about sports? Do you like [5]*them* / *us*, too?
Anika: I love tennis. My favorite player is Serena Williams. [6]*Her* / *She* is amazing!
Thomas: Yes, she is. My friend Paul and I watch tennis all the time, too. Would you like to watch tennis with [7]*her* / *us* some time?
Anika: That sounds great, thanks! I know your friend Paul. I sometimes see [8]*it* / *him* at college.

➤ Go back to page 85.

Grammar Hub

12.1

Countable and uncountable nouns

Countable nouns	Uncountable nouns
bag/bags	**cash**
card/cards	**information**
dollar/dollars	**luggage**
hour/hours	**money**
ticket/tickets	**traffic**
train/trains	**water**

- A countable noun is a noun we can count – we can have one, two or more.

  __one__ passport *__two__ passports*
  I don't have __a passport__.
  My friend has __two passports__ – he's American and Italian.

- We can't count uncountable nouns.

  water NOT ~~one water, two waters~~
  What's happened? There's water all over the floor!

- We use a singular verb with uncountable nouns.

  Money is … NOT ~~Money are …~~
  I think money is very important.
  Money isn't important. It's more important to be happy!

- We never use *a* or *an* with uncountable nouns.

  Money … OR The money … OR Some money … NOT ~~A money …~~
  The money for the taxi is on the table.

Be careful!

- Never make an uncountable noun plural. Uncountable nouns do not have plural forms.

  information NOT ~~informations~~

12.2

Present progressive

	Positive	Negative	Question
Present progressive	**I'm taking** my camera with me.	**They aren't staying** in a hotel.	**Is Tina going** skiing?

- You know that we use the present progressive to talk about things happening now (see Unit 8). We can also use the present progressive to talk about the future. In this sentence, the people aren't traveling right now – the trip is in the future.

  We're traveling to France next week.

- We use the present progressive like this to talk about our plans for the future.

  Helga is staying in a hotel. (She booked it last week.)
  The girls are flying to the US. (They have their tickets and passports.)

- We frequently use future time expressions with the present progressive when we are talking about future plans:
  e.g. *tomorrow, next week, soon, in the summer, this evening*.

Be careful!

- You can only use the present progressive for the future if there's a plan.

  I'm watching a soccer game tomorrow. NOT
  ~~I'm winning a soccer game tomorrow.~~

12.1

Countable and uncountable nouns

A Complete the table with words from the box to make pairs of countable and uncountable nouns.

credit cards homework hours luggage music sandwiches ~~traffic~~ water

Countable nouns	Uncountable nouns
cars	[1] *traffic*
bags	[2]
[3]	money
songs	[4]
exercises	[5]
[6]	food
[7]	time
bottles	[8]

B Choose the correct options to complete the sentences.

1 Australian passports *is* / *are* blue. (*are* circled)
2 These exercises *is* / *are* really difficult!
3 The traffic *was* / *were* bad today.
4 The sun *is* / *are* too hot today!
5 The taxi *was* / *were* late and we missed our flight!
6 The cash *isn't* / *aren't* here!
7 The music *was* / *were* great at the party!
8 The food *is* / *are* on the table.

C If the phrase in bold is correct, put a check mark (✓). If it's wrong, put an (✗).

1 I want **an information** about train times, please. *✗*
2 We made **a plan** to meet tomorrow. ____
3 Do you like **a music**? ____
4 I don't have **a credit card**. ____
5 Do you want **a sandwich**? ____
6 Do you want **a food**? ____
7 Here's **a bag** for the plane. ____
8 Do you have **a luggage** for the plane? ____

D Complete the sentences with the words in the box and choose C (countable noun) or U (uncountable noun).

cash dollars information plane ticket

1 We took a ________ from Madrid in Spain to Bogotá in Colombia. *C* / *U*
2 I changed my euros into ________ at the airport. *C* / *U*
3 I asked for some ________ about the trip at the train station. *C* / *U*
4 I need some ________. Some stores don't take credit cards. *C* / *U*
5 I got a(n) ________ for the train to Ankara. *C* / *U*

➤ Go back to page 91.

12.2

Present progressive

A Are these sentences about what's happening now or a plan in the future? Choose (N) for Now or (P) for Plan.

1 Ssh! The children are doing their homework. *N* / *P* (*N* circled)
2 We're flying to Paris next week. *N* / *P*
3 I'm staying in a tent and it's cold! *N* / *P*
4 We're meeting at the train station. Don't be late! *N* / *P*
5 Gemma is waiting to get on her flight. She's bored. *N* / *P*
6 What time are we meeting Lauren? *N* / *P*

B Complete the conversation using the present progressive. Use the words in parentheses to help you.

Axel: What [1] ________ (*you / do*) this summer?
Ben: [2] ________ (*I / go*) on a sightseeing vacation in Istanbul.
Axel: Great! Who [3] ________ (*you / go*) with?
Ben: [4] ________ (*I / go*) with my sister. She's a photographer.
Axel: [5] ________ (*she / take*) her camera?
Ben: No, [6] ________ (*she / be*). She doesn't like working when she's on vacation.

C Complete the sentences and questions with the correct present progressive form of the verbs in parentheses.

1 *Are you traveling* (*you/travel*) by train or by bus?
2 My parents ________ (*not/take*) a lot of luggage with them.
3 Alexander ________ (*go*) skiing next week.
4 Where ________ (*you/stay*)?
5 The students ________ (*go*) sightseeing around Kyoto tomorrow.
6 We ________ (*camp*) in the mountains for the summer.
7 What ________ (*Ali/take*) with him on vacation?
8 Sara ________ (*not/work*) next week.

➤ Go back to page 93.

Vocabulary Hub

1.2 Jobs

Match the words in the box with the pictures.

an actor   a builder   a chef   a musician   a photographer   a police officer   a receptionist   a sales person   a soccer player   a writer

1 ______________

2 ______________

3 ______________

4 ______________

5 ______________

6 ______________

7 ______________

8 ______________

9 ______________

10 ______________

➤ Go back to page 4.

2.1 Nationalities

Look at the flags. Use *-an*, *-ian*, *-ese* or *-ish* to write the nationality for each country.

Algeria

____

Chile

____

Denmark

____

Italy

____

Lebanon

____

Morocco

____

Russia

____

Scotland

____

Venezuela

____

Vietnam

____

➤ Go back to page 10.

2.2 Numbers 11–100

Write these words in numbers.

a thirty-seven <u>37</u>
b ninety-two ______
c twenty-four ______
d fifty-one ______
e eighty-three ______
f sixty-five ______
g forty-six ______
h seventy-nine ______

➤ Go back to page 12.

3.1 Objects and colors

Match the words with the colors.

black blue brown green gray red white yellow

a ______ b ______ c ______ d ______ e ______ f ______ g ______ h ______

➤ Go back to page 18.

4.1 Daily activities

Look at the pictures and complete the phrases with the verbs in the box.

go (x2) have read talk watch

1 ______ breakfast

2 ______ home

3 ______ to bed

4 ______ TV / a movie

5 ______ to my friends/family

6 ______ a book

➤ Go back to page 26.

Vocabulary Hub

5.2 Food and meals

A Look at the pictures. Practice the words with a partner.

1 ______

banana

pear

orange

grapes

2 ______

tomato

broccoli

cucumber

onion

3 ______

tea

milk

juice

water

4 ______

chocolate

chips

peanuts

cookies

B Label the food groups.

drinks fruits snacks vegetables

C Add two more words to each group. Tell the class.

➤ Go back to page 36.

6.2 Furniture and rooms

A Look at the picture. Write the correct word next to each number.

coffee table couch fridge mirror oven rug shower toilet

1	______	5	______
2	______	6	______
3	______	7	______
4	______	8	______

B Label the rooms (a–c) with the words in the box.

bathroom kitchen living room

➤ Go back to page 44.

7.1 Abilities

Look at the pictures. Use the verbs *make*, *play*, *ride* and *speak* to make phrases about abilities.

make play ride speak

1 ____ride____ a bicycle

2 __________ a cake

3 __________ Chinese

4 __________ an omelette

5 __________ Spanish

6 __________ tennis

7 __________ the piano

8 __________ a horse

➤ Go back to page 51.

8.2 Clothes

Match the words in the box with the pictures.

cap coat dress hat jacket jeans pants shirt shoes skirt suit sweater

1 __________

2 __________

3 __________

4 __________

5 __________

6 __________

7 __________

8 __________

9 __________

10 __________

11 __________

12 __________

➤ Go back to page 60.

Vocabulary Hub

11.1 Recreational activities

Complete the table with the recreational activities in the box.

get takeout food | go to a concert | go to a soccer game | go to a restaurant | ~~listen to music~~ | watch soccer on TV

Going out	Staying in	Both
		listen to music

➤ Go back to page 82.

11.2 Entertainment

Match the words in the box with the pictures.

~~action~~ | baseball | basketball | classical | comedy | horror | jazz | pop | rock | sci-fi | soccer | tennis

Types of music

1 ____________

2 ____________

3 ____________

4 ____________

Types of sports

1 ____________

2 ____________

3 ____________

4 ____________

Types of movies

1 action

2 ____________

3 ____________

4 ____________

➤ Go back to page 85.

12.1 Travel

Match the phrases to the pictures.

by bike | by bus | by car | by plane | by taxi | by train | by trolley | on foot

a ____________

b ____________

c ____________

d ____________

e ____________

f ____________

g ____________

h ____________

➤ Go back to page 90.

12.2 Types of vacations

A Match the words with the pictures.

a camera | a guidebook | skiing goggles | skis | a snorkel | a stove | sunglasses | a tent

a ____________

b ____________

c ____________

d ____________

e ____________

f ____________

g ____________

h ____________

B Choose two things from Exercise A that you use when you go on …

- a beach vacation: ____________, ____________
- a camping vacation: ____________, ____________
- a sightseeing vacation: ____________, ____________
- a skiing vacation: ____________, ____________

➤ Go back to page 93.

Communication Hub

6.2

Student A

Look at your picture. Your partner has a similar picture but there are eight differences. Ask questions to find the differences.

A: Is there a bed in your picture?

B: Yes, there is.

➤ Go back to page 44.

1.2

Student B

A PLAN Imagine this woman is your friend. Complete the information about her with your own ideas.

First name ____________

Last name ____________

Country ____________

City ____________

Job ____________

B PREPARE Prepare to introduce your friend to your partner. Practice by yourself.

This is a picture of my friend. Her name is Cristina. She's from …

C PRACTICE Work in pairs. Listen to your partner's introduction.

D REPEAT Introduce your friend to your partner.

➤ Go back to page 5.

10.2

Group B

A PREPARE Read the survey. You need to write one person's name for each sentence and find out extra information.

B PLAN Write the questions you need to ask for each item.

Did you win a prize or a competition at school?
What kind of competition did you win?

Find someone who:

1 … wanted to be a doctor when they were a child
Why?

2 … won a prize or a competition at school.
What?

3 … collected something when they were young.
What?

4 … had a favorite toy when they were a child.
What?

C PRACTICE Walk around the classroom and ask questions. Write the names and the answers.

A: Did you want to be a doctor when you were a child?
B: Yes, I did.
A: Why did you want to be a doctor?

D REPORT Work with someone from Group A. Tell them what you found out.

Paolo won an art competition when he was at school. He won first prize.

➤ Go back to page 77.

3.1

Coatroom attendant

Turn your back, or leave the room, for two minutes.

You are a coatroom attendant. The others are customers.

Look for their objects and check that you have the correct things. Ask about:

1 the name of the object/objects (hat, bag, headphones, etc)

2 the color/colors (red, blue, black and white, gray and brown)

Remember: *this/these*.

Change roles and repeat.

Are these your glasses?

➤ Go back to page 19.

12.2

Student B

You are the presenter of a radio show. You are going to call your partner and tell them they are the winner of a vacation. Write notes about what to say:

Vacation type: skiing

Place: mountains, Switzerland

Start: next Thursday

How long: ten days

Hello, is that …?
Congratulations! You are the winner.

➤ Go back to page 93.

Communication Hub

9.2

Group B

A PREPARE Complete the sentences with the past tense of the verbs in the box. Then choose the correct information (a, b or c) to complete the sentences.

design receive travel walk

1 Ibn Battuta ________________ from Morocco to China in the …

a 10th century. b 12th century. c 14th century.

2 Gabriel García Márquez ________________ the Nobel Prize in Literature in …

a 1972. b 1982. c 1992.

3 Neil Armstrong ________________ on the moon in …

a 1959. b 1969. c 1979.

4 Steve Jobs and Steve Wozniak ________________ the first personal computers in …

a 1966. b 1976. c 1986.

B PRACTICE Read your sentences to Group A. They will check your answers.

C PRACTICE Listen to Group A's sentences. Check their answers.

Correct sentences:

1 Larry Page and Sergey Brin **started** the company Google in **1998**.

2 John Couch Adams **discovered** the planet Neptune in **1846**.

3 William Shakespeare **lived** in England in the **16th century**.

4 Malala Yousafzai **received** the Nobel Peace Prize in **2014**.

➤ Go back to page 69.

6.2

Student B

A PREPARE You want to rent a room from your partner. Read the description of what you need. Write five questions to ask your partner.

- a table. *Is there a table?*
- lamps.
- a large window.
- the internet.
- near museums and theaters.
- near restaurants.

B SPEAK Answer your partner's questions. Use the information in the advertisement.

Your room:

- Comfortable room in quiet area.
- 10 minutes from train station.
- Near stores and restaurants.
- Has a bed, desk, chair and lamp.

$250 per week.

C REPEAT Ask your partner questions about their room. Find out if it is the right place for you.

A: Can I ask about the room for rent?
B: Yes, of course. How can I help you?
A: Is it near museums and theaters?
B: Yes, it is.

D REPORT Tell the class about the room.

I like / don't like my partner's room because …

➤ Go back to page 45.

4.2
Student B

A PREPARE Look at the picture. Write questions to find the missing information.

1 what / called ______________________________?
2 where / live ______________________________?
3 where / go / in the fall ______________________________?
4 where / go / in the spring ______________________________?
5 how far / go *How far do they go every year*______________________________?

B DISCUSS Ask your partner the questions in Exercise A. Complete the missing information.

C DISCUSS Read the information about Arctic terns. Answer your partner's questions.

Name: Arctic terns
Where: The Arctic and the Antarctic
When: In August or September they go to the Antarctic. In May or June they go to the Arctic.
How far: About 44,000 miles per year (70,800 kilometers)

➤ Go back to page 29.

8.1
Student B

Look at the instructions below.

- Look at the picture.
- Describe the people and what they are doing to your partner.
- Listen to your partner's description of their picture.
- Find six differences.

➤ Go back to page 59.

6.2

Student B

Look at your picture. Your partner has a similar picture but there are eight differences. Ask questions to find the differences.

A: Is there a bed in your picture?

B: Yes, there is.

➤ Go back to page 44.

2.2

Student B

A PREPARE Read the information. What questions can you ask to find the missing information?

Write your questions here.

1 *Where's Victor Moretti from?* ?
2 ____________ ?
3 ____________ ?
4 ____________ ?
5 ____________ ?
6 ____________ ?
7 ____________ ?
8 ____________ ?

B PRACTICE Ask your partner questions to complete the information about each person.

a

Name	Victor Moretti
Country	1 ________
Age	28
Job	2 ________

b

Name	3 ________
Country	Japan
Age	4 ________
Job	Doctor

c

Name	Dev Gupta
Country	5 ________
Age	42
Job	6 ________

d

Name	Zehra Yilmaz
Country	7 ________
Age	8 ________
Job	Computer programmer

➤ Go back to page 13.

12.2

Student A

You are the listener of a radio show. You entered a competition on the radio show's website to win a vacation. Read the information below, then answer your phone and talk to the radio presenter.

- You don't like cold weather.
- You don't have a passport.
- You're a doctor. You're working at the hospital next week.

➤ Go back to page 93.

7.2

Student B

B PREPARE Read the information about this person. Write questions to find the missing information.

UTA ABE and her brother Hifumi are from Japan. Hifumi is very good at [1] ______ and is a world champion. Uta is good at [2] ______. She's the 2017 Junior World Champion. Hifumi and Uta are the winners of [3] ______.

1 What is Hifumi good at?
2 What ...?
3 What ...?

C DISCUSS Now ask your partner questions to complete the missing information. Answer your partner's questions.

D REPEAT Repeat with the information below.

ALISTAIR BROWNLEE is from [1] ______. He is good at triathlons – three events in one race. He can [2] ______ – and he's fast! His brother is good at triathlons, too. His brother's name is [3] ______. They both have Olympic medals.

➤ Go back to page 53.

Audio scripts

Welcome

The alphabet, Exercise C

0.5 1 Carlos. C – a – r – l – o – s

2 Hassan. H – a – s – s – a – n

3 Erica. E – r – i – c – a

Unit 1

Lesson 1.1 Listening, Exercise B

1.2 **R = Receptionist L = Lisa**

R: Good morning! Can I help you?

L: Hello! Yes, I'd like some English lessons, please.

R: Of course! What's your name?

L: My first name is Lisa, L – i – s – a, and my last name is Fuentes, F – u – e – n – t – e – s.

R: Thank you. Where are you from?

L: I'm from Spain.

R: Are you from Madrid?

L: No, I'm not. I'm from Bilbao.

R: What's your phone number?

L: 0764 729 3387.

R: OK … Now, let's find a class for you …

Unit 2

Lesson 2.2 Listening, Exercise A

2.6 **P = Pete K = Kara A = Angelo M = Maria L = Leila H = Hana**

Conversation 1

P: Hi, Kara! How are you?

K: Hi, Pete! Fine, thanks.

P: Are you free this evening?

K: No, I'm not. I have my Spanish guitar class this evening.

P: Oh, OK! Who's your teacher?

K: Our teacher is Ms. Sanchez.

P: Really? Where's she from?

K: She's from Argentina.

Conversation 2

A: Hi! Is this classroom 12B?

M: Yes, it is. Are you here for the Arabic class, too?

A: Yes, I am. I'm a new student.

M: Great! What's your name?

A: My name's Angelo!

M: Hello, Angelo. I'm Maria. Nice to meet you.

A: Nice to meet you, too.

Conversation 3

L: Good afternoon! Are you a teacher here, too?

H: Yes, I am! My name's Hana. I'm the yoga teacher.

L: Nice to meet you! My name's Leila. I'm the Arabic class teacher.

H: Nice to meet you! When's your class?

L: Now! Bye!

H: OK, bye!

Unit 3

Lesson 3.1 Listening, Exercise A

3.3 **C = Customer CA = Coatroom attendant**

C: Hello. Can I have my coat, please?

CA: Yes. What's your ticket number?

C: It's 42.

CA: 42, OK … here you are.

C: Sorry, that isn't my coat. That's a red coat. My coat's blue.

CA: Oh, sorry. Uh … Is this your coat?

C: No! My coat is blue. That coat is green.

CA: Oh, yes … Is this your coat?

C: No. My coat is blue! That coat is black.

CA: This one?

C: Yes, that's it.

CA: Here you go.

C: Thank you. And can I have my bags, please?

CA: Bags?

C: Yes, there are two bags. One is green and the other one is white.

CA: Are these your bags?

C: No! Those bags are red and blue. My bags are green and white!

CA: Sorry! Sorry! Are these your bags?

C: Yes!

CA: Here you go.

C: Thank you.

Unit 4

Lesson 4.1 Listening, Exercise B

4.2 **P = Presenter A = Astrid M = Magne**

P: My life … the lighthouse keepers.

A: Hello. My name's Astrid. I'm a lighthouse keeper. I live and work in a lighthouse.

M: Hi. I'm Magne. I'm Astrid's husband. I also live and work in the lighthouse. We work in the same place.

A: But we don't work at the same time. I get up very early – at five o'clock in the morning! I start work at five fifteen, and I finish at one thirty in the afternoon.

M: I don't work in the morning. I start work at one thirty in the afternoon, and I finish work late – at nine forty-five in the evening.

A: I relax and watch TV in the afternoon but I don't watch TV in the evening. I make something to eat and then I go to bed at eight o'clock.

M: I watch TV or read a book in the evening. I go to bed at one o'clock in the morning and I get up late at 11 o'clock in the morning.

Unit 5

Lesson 5.1 Listening, Exercise A

5.2 **I = Interviewer W = Woman M = Man**

I: Hi! Do you have a minute? I'd like to ask you some questions.

W: OK. What's it about?

I: It's about how you relax in your free time.

W: OK!

M: Sure!

I: Thanks! Do you work near here?

W: Yes, we both work in the offices over there.

I: Great! Question one: what do you do on your lunch break?

M: Um … I have lunch at my desk; I don't have time to take a break.

W: Yes, he works all the time! He doesn't even take coffee breaks!

I: Do you go to the gym on your lunch break?

W: No, I don't. My friend has a gym at her office and she goes there on her lunch break.

I: That sounds good. Does she go to the gym every day?

W: No, she doesn't. She goes about twice a week.

I: OK. The next question is: what do you do to relax after work?

W: I usually go home and cook a meal, and watch TV.

M: Yeah, I go running after work. After that, I go home and take a bath.

I: OK. Question three: what do you do to relax on the weekend?

W: Umm … well … I go running …

M: Yeah, she goes running and I go food shopping. She doesn't like food shopping!

W: Then I relax in the evening. I cook a nice meal and watch a movie on TV.

I: That's great. Thanks for your time today. Please take a free one-day pass to our new gym!

W: Ooh! Thanks …!

M: Thank you …!

Unit 6

Lesson 6.2 Vocabulary, Exercise B

6.4 **M = Martin**

M: Hi everyone, my name's Martin and I'm looking for someone to rent my room. As you can see, there's a desk and two chairs. There's a big closet. You can put your clothes in there. There's a bookshelf. All my books are on it right now. There's a small table with a lamp on it next to the bed. Oops, my clock is under the bed. Sorry about that! Those are a couple of my pictures on the wall. And there's a window with a nice view of the yard. All this for 200 dollars a month!

Lesson 6.2 Listening, Exercise C

6.5 **R = Realtor M = Man**

R: Hi! This is New York City Rentals. How can I help you?

M: Hello. I'd like some information about the studio for rent on East 23rd Street.

R: Sure! No problem. Let's see. That's number 25B, the studio? What would you like to know?

M: Are there any buses on that street?

R: Yes, there are. It's about a 10-minute walk to the bus stop.

M: OK. Are there any stores nearby?

R: Yes, there are. There's a grocery store on the corner and there are a lot of restaurants nearby.

M: Is there a living room and a bedroom?

R: No, it's a studio. There's only one room.

M: Oh, I see. What about the furniture? What's in the room? Are there any chairs?

R: No, there aren't. There are some bookshelves, a lamp and a bed. That's all. It's a small studio …

M: There's no desk and no chair. Hmm. Is there a large window?

R: Yes, there's a large window with a view of the park.

M: Is there a bathroom?

R: Yes, there is. There's a small bathroom with a shower, but no bathtub.

M: Is there a kitchen?

R: No, there isn't. It's just one room!

M: No kitchen and no bathtub, and you want $2,000 a month! You must be joking!

Unit 7

Lesson 7.2 Listening, Exercise B

7.2 **O = Oliver C = Carrie**

O: Welcome to *The People Show*. Today's special person is a very interesting young musician. His name's Sheku Kanneh-Mason and he's from Nottingham in the UK. Tell us more, Carrie.

C: Hi, Oliver. Sheku Kanneh-Mason's an amazing musician. He's the winner of the 2016 BBC Young Musician of the Year Award, and he was a musician at Prince Harry and Meghan Markle's wedding in May 2018.

O: What instrument does he play?

C: He plays the cello. But Sheku isn't the only musician in his family. He has six brothers and sisters, and they're all wonderful musicians.

O: Six? Wow! So, there are seven children in the Kanneh-Mason family?

C: That's right. Braimah is Sheku's brother. He plays the violin. Isata is Sheku's sister, and she plays the piano. They are all students at London's Royal Academy of Music. Sheku also has four younger sisters.

O: What instruments do they play?

C: Konya and Aminata play the violin, and Jeneba and Mariatu play the cello. These four can all also play the piano.

O: Are they students at the Royal Academy of Music, as well?

C: No, they don't go there – not yet anyway. They're too young right now.

O: So, is everyone in the Kanneh-Mason family a musician?

C: No, they aren't. Sheku's parents' names are Kadiatu and Stuart. They don't play any musical instruments.

O: I'm not surprised. It's difficult to find the time to play an instrument when you have seven children!

Unit 8

Lesson 8.1 Listening, Exercise C

8.1 **A = Officer A B = Officer B**

A: Can you see the man?

B: Yes. I'm watching him now.

A: What's he doing?

B: He's having lunch.

A: Is he talking to anyone?

B: No, he isn't. He's by himself.

A: Is he in a café?

B: No, he's sitting on a bench. He's eating a sandwich and drinking coffee.

B: OK … he's finishing his lunch.

A: Where's he going now?

B: He's stopping at the bank.

A: The bank! OK. This is it.

B: Wait. He isn't going to the bank. He's looking at his phone. I think he's reading a message. OK. He's walking. He's going to … the library.

A: The library? OK. Stay with him.

B: He's in the library.

A: Right. What's he doing there?

B: He's talking to someone. She's showing him something.

A: What is it?

B: It's …

A: Yes?

B: It's a book!

A: A book. What's happening now?

B: He's leaving.

A: Stay with him.

B: I can see him.

A: What's he doing?

B: He's going to the bank.

A: The bank! OK. This time … This is it.

B: Wait. He's not going to the bank. He's going to the park.

A: The park? Is he meeting anyone?

B: No, he isn't.

A: Argh. What's he doing?

B: He's lying down. He's taking a nap. I think he's sleeping.

A: What? Are you watching the right man?

B: Yes, I am! He's tall, he has gray hair and he's wearing a green coat.

A: No, that's not him. Our man has a gray coat, not a green coat. You're watching the wrong man. What's that noise?

B: Um … It's coming from the bank.

Unit 9

Lesson 9.1 Listening Exercise B

9.1 **A = Anna Ni = Nick AG = Audio Guide**

A: Oh, who's this? Was she a model?

Ni: Oh, I don't know. Push the button. Let's find out who she was.

AG: Meet Hollywood actor Audrey Hepburn. She was born in Belgium on May 4, 1929. Her movies were very popular in the 1950s and 60s. She wasn't just an actor, she was also a dancer and a model. She was famous for her beautiful clothes!

A: Hey Nick, come here. Look! Why was he famous?

Ni: I don't know. Let's listen.

AG: William Shakespeare was born in Stratford-upon-Avon in England on April 26, 1564. He was a famous writer. He's famous for plays such as Romeo and Juliet, and Hamlet. He wasn't just a writer, he was an actor, too. His plays were very important for the English language. Hundreds of the words we use in English today come from Shakespeare.

Ni: Look over here. I don't know who this is. Do you know?

A: No idea!

AG: Marie Tussaud was born in Strasbourg in France on December 1, 1761. She's now famous for the Madame Tussauds museum in London. Marie Tussaud was very good at making wax models of people and her waxworks were very popular. Photographs weren't common at the time, but Marie Tussaud made a waxwork of herself – was this a type of selfie?

A: That was really interesting! Now, we know who this is! He was President of …

Ni: South Africa!

AG: This famous politician was born in South Africa on July 18, 1918. His name is Nelson Mandela. He was in prison for 27 years. Later, he was president for five years from 1994 to 1999. He was the first black president of South Africa.

Unit 10

Lesson 10.2 Listening, Exercise B

10.3 **P = Presenter J = Janine A = Alfie I = Isabel**

P: In today's podcast, we invited three people to tell us about a family object that has a special meaning for them. Janine, hi and welcome to our podcast. Please tell us about the family object you brought with you today and why it's important to you.

J: Hi! Yes, this silver pocket watch belonged to my great-grandfather. He gave it to his son, and his son gave it to my father – and my father gave it to me when I finished college.

P: So it has a lot of family history. Where did this watch come from? What did your great-grandfather use it for?

J: I think he bought it in the 1880s from a famous watchmaker in New York. He worked on the railroads, and he used this watch every day. He made sure the trains were on time. So that's why this watch reminds me never to be late!

P: That's an amazing story. Thank you! Now, let's talk to Alfie. That looks like a nice camera, Alfie.

A: Thanks. My mother gave it to me. She bought it in the 1970s.

P: It was probably very modern in those days! Did your mother take a lot of photos?

A: Yes, she did. She took a lot of photos of me and my brother when we were young. She gave me the camera on my 16th birthday. That's probably why I became a photographer.

P: That's so interesting. And finally, let's talk to Isabel. This is a beautiful necklace. Did you buy this or did someone give it to you?

I: Actually, these pearls belonged to my grandmother. My grandfather gave them to her on the day they got married. Then, she gave me this necklace when I got married. I loved my grandmother very much. I always think of her when I wear this necklace. That's why the necklace is so important to me.

P: That's wonderful! Thanks so much to all of you for sharing your stories with us today. I'm afraid that's all we have time for today, but don't forget if you have stories to share, upload your photo and a brief description on our website!

Unit 11

Lesson 11.2 Listening, Exercise A

11.5 **I = Interviewer W = Wendy K = Kelly R = Ryan**

I: This is the *Sports Talk* soccer show and I'm at the Olympic Stadium in Berlin for this international friendly game between Germany and Egypt … and as you can hear, there are a lot of people here. They come from all over the world, and many of them are here to see one man: Mo Salah, the soccer superstar from Egypt. Hi! Can I ask you a few questions?

W: Sure. No problem.

I: What's your name?

W: I'm Wendy.

I: Who are you here to see, Wendy?

W: Mo Salah – I'm such a big fan!

I: Why do you like him?

W: I think he's great. I love watching him play. I also like him because he's a nice person. He's always good to his fans.

I: Thanks, Wendy. Hi, can I ask you a few questions?

K: Um … OK.

I: What's your name?

K: Kelly.

I: OK Kelly, what do you think about Mo Salah?

K: Um … My boyfriend likes him. I don't know.

I: Are you a soccer fan?

K: No, I'm not. My boyfriend loves soccer, but I hate it – it's so boring.

I: Oh … OK, well, um … is this your boyfriend?

K: Yeah, that's him.

I: Hello, can I ask you …

R: He's Egyptian and he's amazing and Mohammed's his name.

I: OK, great. So, what's your name?

R: Ryan.

I: So, why are you …

R: Mo Sa–la–la–la–lah! Mo Sa–la–la–la–lah!

I: Why are you a big Mo Salah fan, Ryan?

R: Because he is the number one in the world!

I: Do you watch Mo Salah play a lot?

R: I watch every game he plays – club and country.

I: So, Ryan, what do you think about the other soccer players?

R: I'm not interested in them. I only like Salah!

I: Thanks, Ryan. I hope you enjoy watching the game. Well, the game starts in one hour.

Unit 12

Lesson 12.2 Listening, Exercise C

2.4 **M = Mikey Greene J = Jo**

M: Now listeners, it's three o'clock on Tuesday afternoon and it's time to call this week's competition winner. Have your phone with you – we are calling … now!

J: Hello?

M: Is this Jo?

J: Yes, yes, yes! Is this Mikey?

M: It's Mikey Greene and you're on the radio! Congratulations, Jo – you are this week's competition winner!

J: Wow! That's amazing. I never win anything.

M: Well, you're a winner today.

J: I can't believe it. Me?

M: That's right, Jo. Your prize is a vacation for you and a friend.

J: Wow! I don't usually enter competitions, but I saw the picture on the website of the beach and the ocean, and I thought, 'This is the vacation for me!' I'm so excited.

M: The picture on the website? Oh, right, yeah. Um … that's not a picture of the vacation you're going on.

J: Oh, really?

M: Yes, you're going on a different kind of vacation. But don't worry. It's an amazing vacation.

J: Oh. OK then.

M: Who are you taking with you?

J: I'm taking my friend, Charlotte. She loves going to the beach.

M: That's great, Jo, but just to be clear: you're not going on a beach vacation this time.

J: No beach?

M: Um … no.

J: What kind of vacation is it, Mikey?

M: Well, Jo … it's a camping vacation!

J: Camping. In a tent?

M: That's right. You're going to the countryside, and you're staying in a tent, next to some mountains.

J: Mountains? Charlotte hates walking and she doesn't like cold weather. When are we going?

M: You're going … next Wednesday!

J: Next Wednesday? It's November, Mikey. It's really cold. How long are we going for?

M: It's a two-week vacation, Jo. Isn't that great?

J: Two weeks? In a tent? In the cold?

M: Next to a mountain. That's right, Jo. Have a great time. Bye, Jo. Well listeners, I think Jo's really excited about her vacation. Next week's competition is … a beach vacation in Brazil.

Macmillan Education Limited
4 Crinan Street
London N1 9XW

Companies and representatives throughout the world

American Language Hub Starter Student's Book ISBN 978-0-230-49665-1
American Language Hub Starter Student's Book with Student's App
ISBN 978-0-230-49667-5

Written by Ingrid Wisniewska and Ed Price

First published 2020

Designed by emc design ltd
Illustrated by Daniel Limon (Beehive Illustration) ppvi, 18, 19, 20, 23, 24, 42, 44, 46, 47, 48, 58, 59, 60, 63, 70, 92, 103, 122, 125, 126, 130.
Cover design by Restless
Cover photograph by Getty Images/Valentinrussanov
Picture research by Emily Taylor
Café Hub videos produced by Creative Listening.
Café Hub video scripts written by James and Luke Vyner.

Authors' acknowledgements
Ingrid Wisniewska would like to thank her husband Greg for his constant support and encouragement.

Ed Price would like to give special thanks, always, to Becca and Henry.

The authors and publishers would like to thank the following for permission to reproduce their photographs:

Alamy pp32, 36(i,l), 127(12.1.a), Aflo Co. Ltd p53(tr), Galyna Andrushko p29a, Aurora Photos p50(c), Blickwinkel p29(tr), Pat Canova p76(L_c), Piero Cruciatti p10(tl), Lev Dolgachov p68(1), Vadym Drobot p61(a), Endless Travel p66(Tussaud), Bella Falk p2(bl), Galopin p29(d), Rostislav Glinsky p127(12.1.b), Granger Historical Picture Archive p72(tml), Heritage Image Partnership Ltd p74(b), Jiri Hubatka p20(2), imageBROKER pp50(a), 51(2), Interfoto p67, John Warburton-Lee Photography p36(Sara), Kamila Koziol p127(12.2.e), Dennis MacDonald p72(tmr), Mauritius Images p66(Shakespeare), Peter Mayer p125(8.2.2), Photopat p90(7), The Picture Art Collection p75(tl), Alex Robinson p10(2), Alan Schein p90(4), Sho Tamura/Aflo Sport p133(t), Tetra Images p82(Agnes), Viktorus p40(3), Visuals Stock p76(V_b), Westend61 p34(2), Jan Wlodarczyk p26(tr); **Artifacts Images** p90(3); **Blend Images**/Steve Smith p125(8.2.9); **BrandX** pp24(tl), 45, 124(pear); **Caiaimage**/Great Images p20(3); **Corbis** pp96(tl), 127(12.2.h); **Decisive Images** p125(8.2.4); **Getty** Images pp2(tr), 4(8), 6(4,7,8), 34(7), 34(8), 36(buffet), 61(SH_b, bl), 62–63(background), 66(background), 70–71(background), 78(bl), 82(a), 82(Lee, Frieda), 90(2), 95(br), 123(4,5,6), 124(orange, broccoli, milk, water, nuts), 125(7.1.6, 7.1.8), 126(cmr), 127(12.2.a), AFP pp10(tml), 72(tr), 10'000 Hours pp83(br), 129(tr), Age fotostock p42, Dmytro Aksonov p64(a), Ursula Alter p40(2), Anadolu Agency p66(Hepburn), Subodh Agnihotri p94(b), Ann Ronan Picture Library/Heritage Images p74(l), Thomas Barwick p51(4), Ben Pipe Photography p34(br), Alistair Berg p82(2), Margarita Almpanezou p94(a), Nick Ballon p126(bml), Michael Blann p23(cr), Blend Images/Dmitry Ageev p125(8.2.6), Blend Images/Chris Clor p34(4), Blend Images/KidStock p82(1), Blend Images/Patrick Lienin p92(c), Blend Images/Jeremy Woodhouse/Holly Wilmeth p9, Biddiboo p77, Blue Jean Images p122(3), Brand X p59(8), Nick Brundle p2(tl), Gary Burchell p34(3), Caiaimage pp26(d), 79(party), Caiaimage/Tom Merton p7(br), Caiaimage/Chris Ryan p4(5), Helen Cathcart p61(SH_a), Cavan Images p76(V_c), Petar Chernaev p59(1), Razvan Ciuca p73, Corbis p61(b), Corbis/Robbie Jack p10(1), Derek Croucher p127(12.1.e), Cultura RF pp36(Davide), p50(b), 70(tl), 79(hairdresser) 82(3,4), 125(7.1.1), Nick David pp4(b), 51(f), Peter Dazeley p6(6), Steve Debenport p12(2), Den-belitsky pp38–39(background), DigitalVision p125(7.1.3), 126(tml), DigitalVision/Punchstock p68(7), Dougal Waters Photography Ltd p88, Dan Dunkley p122(1), E+ pp40(1), 82(b), 122(6), 123(2), Eclipse_images p59(7), EyeEm pp2(bl), 6(3), 30–31(background), 25, 127(12.2.c), EyeEm/Marco Agnoletti pp86–87(background), EyeEm/Pinghung Chen p71(br), EyeEm/Urs Flueeler pp54–55(background), EyeEm/Zuzana Gajdosikova p40(4), EyeEm/Bill Green p94(d), EyeEm/Bruno Guerreiro pp94–95(background), EyeEm /Nathan Motoyama p71(tl), EyeEm/Classen Rafael p51(a), EyeEm/Tori Seubert p51(5), EyeEm/Artem Varnitsin p 59(4), Fcafotodigital p36(c, tr), FilmMagic p85(tl), Filmstudio p51(c), First Light pp20(tl), 122(10), Flashpop pp13(b), 132(b), David Freund p128, fStop p90(1), Charley Gallay/Stringer p85(bl), David Clapp Photography p126(bmr), Eleonora Galli p79(beach), Tony Garcia p123(1), Steve Glass p61(d), Kodiak Greenwood p127(12.1.g), Jorg Greuel p95(bl), Hadynyah pp28–29, Hero Images pp3, 4(6,7), 15(bl), 34(bl), 59(2), 69, Heimsmyndir/Stígur Már Karlsson p68(tr), Chris Hepburn p95(tl), Nicolas Herrbach p4(1), Timothy Hiatt p10(tmr), Justin Horrocks p76(V_d), Icon Sport p85(cr), The Image Bank pp27, 33, 34(6), 125(8.2.11), Image Source pp5, 64(br) 125(7.1.2, 7.1.7, 8.2.8), iStockphoto pp26(c), 28(a–d), 29(b), 36(e,j), 71(bl), 80, 90(5,6), 92(b,d), 92–93(background), 96(tr), 124(chips, cookies), 125(7.1.5, 8.2.7), 126(tl), Gavriel Jecan p131, Jetta Productions Inc pp13(c), 132(c), Johner RF p79(picnic), Julian Elliott Photography p95(tr), John Lamb p122(4), Letizia Le Fur p125(8.2.1), Lee Pei Ling pp6–7(background), Warren Little p53(br), Lonely Planet Images pp43(tr), 96(bl), Glenn Losack p65, Peter Lourenco p21, MackoFlower p36(tmr), David Madison pp22–23(background), Maskot pp13(a), 12(1), 68(5,6), 82(5), 132(a), Simon McGill p30(takeaway cup), Chris McKay p126(tmr), Mint Images p6(1), Donald Miralle p133(b), Abel Mitja Varela p20(4), Moment RF pp29(c), 40(cm), MoMo Productions p51(e), Mondenkind p83(emojis), Monkeybusinessimages p26(b), Tara Moore p26(a), Kelvin Murray pp68(3), 75(b), Aleksandar Nakic p4(2), Jekaterina Nikitina p20(1), Gary John Norman p123(3), NurPhoto p84(b), OJO Images p51(b), James O'Neil p89, onfilm p127(12.1.d), Steve Outram p6(2), Cecilia Pensini p125(8.2.3), PeopleImages pp51(3), 76(br), 79(tr), Perspectives p61(SH_c), PhotoDisc p36(g), Photolibrary pp36(tm), 43(bl), 125(7.1.4), Photographer's Choice p36(k), Photononstop p90(8), Steve Prezant p15(br), Robert Harding World Imagery p1, Marc Romanelli pp12(3), 93(br), RooM RF pp40(5), 94(c), 125(8.2.5), 127(12.2.b), RonTech2000 p71(tr), Clive Rose p84(inset), Science Photo Library RF p126(br), Sequya p54(image on book), Sergione Infuso p11, Shironosov pvi, Jordan Siemens p127(12.1.h), Silent Resilience Photography p68(2), Robin Skjoldborg pp13(d), 132(d), skynesher p126(cml), SolisImages p4(3), SolStock pp48, 62(b), Alexander Spatari p79(brunch), Dave Stamboulis p71(mr), Stone Sub pp59(5), 81, 126(bl), Harald Sund pp78–79(background), Taxi p82(6), Tetra images pp6(5), 122(7), Ron Thomas p95(cm), Thomas M. Barwick INC p34(5), Nicola Tree p51(1), Todor Tsvetkov p24(tr), UIG p74(r), Bernd Vogel p122(9), Art Wager pp46–47(background), Jodie Wallis p129(b), Westend61 pp4(4), 34(1), 51(6,d), 61(c), 79(skating), 125(8.2.10), Westend61 p126(cr), Westend61/Jo Kirchherr p127(12.2.d), Wireimage/Sarahphotogirl p49, Peter Zelei p68(4); **Hero Images** pp64(b), 76(V_a); **Hill Street Studios** p122(8); **Lisa Payne Photography** p124(juice); **LWA**/Dann Tardif p68(8); **iStockphoto** pp35, 36(h,d,f), 37(Natalia), 71(ml), 122(2), Wandersmann/Getty Images p127(12.1.f); **Macmillan Education Ltd** pp122(Russia), 124(tea), Paul Bricknell pp36(a), 124(banana, grapes); **Microzoa** p36(b); **Monkeybusinessimages** p126(cl); **PlainPicture**/Elektrons 08 p17, Steven Kazlowski p57, Jason Langley photography p41; **People Images** p125(8.2.12); **Photodisc** Bruce Leighty pp127(12.1.c), p127(12.2.f); **Scheifoto**/Espen Gresvik Schei p10(tr); **Shutterstock**/20th Century Fox/Kobal/REX pp90–91(b), Grisha Bruev p76(L_a), Hauke-Christian Dittrich/EPA/REX p66(Mandela), Imagine China/REX p74(t), Guy Levy/BAFTA/REX p52, Mars0hod p96(br), Monkey Business/REX p59(6), Volis61 p76(L_b), Roman Voloshyn p126(tr), Watcharapong Saiboot pp14–15(background); **Superstock** pp72(tl), 92(tl, a), 122(all flags ex Russia); **Thinkstock** pp30(cup&saucer), 40(6), 122(5), 124(onion, chocolate), 127(12.2.g); **Up the Resolution** p124(tomato, cucumber); **Westend61**/Marco Govel p59(3).

Commissioned photographs by Creative Listening pp6, 7, 14, 15, 22, 23, 30, 31, 38, 39, 46, 47, 54, 55, 62, 63, 71, 78, 79, 86, 87, 94, 95.

Printed and bound in Uruguay

2024

37